JESUS: A PROFILE

✛

JESUS

✛ ✛ ✛

A PROFILE

✛

Alan Watson

The University of Georgia Press
ATHENS & LONDON

© 1998 by the University of Georgia Press
Athens, Georgia 30602
All rights reserved
Designed by Kathi Dailey Morgan
Set in Bembo and Optima
by G & S Typesetters, Inc.
Printed and bound by McNaughton & Gunn, Inc.
The paper in this book meets the guidelines for
permanence and durability of the Committee
on Production Guidelines for Book Longevity
of the Council on Library Resources.

Printed in the United States of America
98 99 00 01 02   C   5 4 3 2 1
Library of Congress Cataloging in Publication Data
Watson, Alan.
Jesus : a profile / Alan Watson.
p.   cm.
Includes bibliographical references and index.
ISBN 0-8203-1970-8 (alk. paper)
1. Jesus Christ—Psychology.   I. Title.
BT590.P9W37   1998
232.9'03 —dc21   97-37854

British Library Cataloging in Publication Data available

For Michael Hoeflich

✠

CONTENTS

✠ ✠ ✠

✠

PREFACE

✠ ✠ ✠

This book has developed from previous works of mine: *Jesus and the Jews: the Pharisaic Tradition in John* (Athens, Ga., 1995); *The Trial of Jesus* (Athens, Ga., 1995); *Jesus and the Law* (Athens, Ga., 1996); *The Trial of Stephen: the First Christian Martyr* (Athens, Ga., 1996). For these my main interest was law in action in the traditions of the lives of Jesus and his immediate followers. But inevitably I had to take a stance on wider issues: the sources for the narrative in John, the relative coherence of the various Gospels, in order to establish the most plausible traditions for Jesus.

Inevitably, too, my earlier books drove me to site the law in action in the context of the life of Jesus and his contemporaries, followers or not. This book resulted from that. Some chapters derive in great measure from my earlier works. My book provides a mere sketch of the subordinate issues.[1] I have no wish to plot an exact chronology of Jesus' life or fix the names of the twelve disciples. Many have written on the life of Jesus or have sought to elucidate how much can be known. The characteristic of this book is the emphasis on Jesus' personality: what he thought himself to be, and how he was perceived by others. Jesus was a Jew of Galilee, the main part of whose life was lived in the first century, but he was not typical of his place or time. The background should not be allowed to have pride of place. In this context what is most important to me is what makes Jesus different from others. Also I am not so much seeking to establish the truth as overall plausibility.[2] Accordingly, at no point will I pronounce on the historical truth of Jesus' miracles of exorcism and healing and his natural miracles. My concern is with their place in traditions about Jesus.

On purpose I have kept citations to modern authors to a minimum to allow my argument to appear most clearly. On the other hand, to establish the accuracy (I hope) of my argument, I cite and extensively quote the original sources.

✛

ACKNOWLEDGMENTS

✛   ✛   ✛

Bobbie Epting, Steven Friedell, Ranon Katzoff, Geoffrey Miller, and Olivia Robinson read my complete manuscript with kindly but critical eyes to my great profit. Sherri Mauldin at first, then Gracie Waldrup, cheerfully and carefully typed many drafts. Once again I thank the staff of the University of Georgia Law Library for unfailing support. Likewise again I am deeply in debt to my publisher, Malcolm Call, for his faith in my work, and to Elaine Otto Durham for superb editing.

Indented translations of the Bible are, for the sake of consistency, all from the New Revised Standard Version, but in the succeeding discussion I use my own translation. Translations from the Mishnah are those of Danby.

✠

INTRODUCTION

✠ ✠ ✠

The merest sketch will set the scene. Jesus was born around 6 B.C. and was brought up and lived in Galilee. Judaea and the nearby territories of the Jews had come under Roman control in 63 B.C. but were not then annexed, although they were placed under the supervision of the governor of Syria. Subsequently Augustus, who had been given power to ratify King Herod's will, divided his territories among his three sons, Archelaus, Herod Antipas, and Philip. In A.D. 6 Augustus brought Judaea, Idumaea, and Samaria under direct Roman rule as part of the province of Syria. Peraea and Galilee remained under Herod Antipas as tetrarch and client of Rome and thus were only indirectly controlled by Rome. Accordingly, Jerusalem, which Jesus entered only near the end of his life, was part of the Roman Empire, but Galilee was not.[1]

The historian Josephus, who was born around A.D. 37, claims that from the earliest times the Jews had three philosophies regarding their traditions—those of the Pharisees, the Sadducees, and the Essenes—but that a fourth had been added by Judas and Saddok.[2]

The Pharisees were a self-selecting group in voluntary association with one another. They accepted as law not only the express commandments of God that were set out in Scripture but also all the rules that could be deduced from it in accordance with the accepted modes of legal reasoning. They did not hold the main priestly offices, but they were literate, concerned with law as the guide to the proper life. When a text talks of scribes, we should envisage primarily Pharisees. Their main interests in law were with ritual purity, Sabbath and festival observance, and marriage, precisely the issues that a religious group under foreign domination could use to define itself. They believed in rewards and punishments after death for their behavior in life, as well as resurrection. According to Josephus, their lifestyle and beliefs made them very influential among the townsfolk.[3] They kept themselves apart from others. Though not a political party, their religious stance could make them implacably hostile to certain political decisions.

The Sadducees were, in effect, the aristocrats among the Jews and filled the important priesthoods. The main priests were a closed group, the male descendants of Aaron, and they had the exclusive right of sacrifice. None of them could be barred from the priesthood. No observing Jew could do without them, so they had a respected position even if, as Josephus the Pharisee insists (perhaps with exaggeration), they accomplished little. They accepted as law only that set out in Scripture, and they did not believe in bodily resurrection. As a hereditary group with important functions, the Sadducees were prominent and thus vulnerable to outside aggressors.[4]

The Essenes (who play almost no role in this book) were admired for their virtue. They held their property in common and were much concerned with ritual purity.[5] Josephus's fourth philosophy is probably that of those who after the time of Jesus were known as Zealots. They believed in God as their sole master and leader, and so they were in opposition to the Romans as an occupying force.[6] Adherence to any of these philosophies, except that of the Sadducees, involved a great commitment. Most Jews, no doubt, would be relatively lax in their religious observances and conform to none of the four philosophies.

The Pharisees tended to despise Galileans, whom they regarded as ignorant.[7] All the more would they be reluctant to see Jesus as the Messiah. Not only was he a Galilean but he spent his ministry in the countryside and small towns.

Messianism was in the air. There was more than one view of the Messiah, but the most important was that he would be a descendant of David, a political figure who drives out the foreign oppressor and returns the dispersed Jews to Israel.[8] Accordingly, he would be an enemy of the Romans.

We have four main accounts of the life of Jesus in the Gospels, and each varies from the others.[9] John in particular differs from the Synoptics. In my previous works I tried to reach conclusions about the plausibility of each account, and I hope here to spare the reader much of the argument. I concluded that for the life of Jesus, John was unreliable unless it could be confirmed by other evidence. The final redactor of Jesus' life understood little about Judaism: what is accurate in John derives from its sources. Mark, I found, gave the most plausible account resting on early traditions. The substance and structure are deeply rabbinical but have been shaped for early Christian propaganda and liturgical purposes. For the plausibility of Mark, I lay no stress on its being the earliest of the surviving Gospels. Matthew, though famed for its rabbinical structure, is actually much less so. At times, when dependent on Mark, its author weakens the force of rabbinism in Mark. Again, Matthew's account of Jesus' trial cannot be squeezed into a plausible scenario, and that Matthew's historical sense is lacking is shown by the impossibility of the account of Jesus' birth and infancy. Much the same can be said about the evangelist Luke. When the Gospel of Luke and Acts (by the same author) seem to be historically plausible, this is because of the reliability of their sources. But the evangelist has no feel for historical reality.[10]

Thus, for this book I shall rely most heavily on Mark. I shall not start with a justification. Much of the argument for believing his account the most plausible and the most rabbinic will emerge in the various chapters. But to finish this introductory sketch I want to produce two episodes that otherwise have no place in the book but that may begin to indicate the strength of rabbinic influence in Mark.

My first example is Jesus' prayer in Gethsemane after the Passover meal. The general view is that the prayer is in two antithetical parts—wish, surrender—and is the quintessence of all prayer. And so it is in Matthew 26.39: "My Father, if it is possible, let this cup pass from me: yet not what I want but what you want." And in Luke 22.42: "Father, if you are willing, remove this cup from me: yet, not my will but yours be done." But in Mark 14.36 the prayer is in three parts: "Abba, Father, for you all things are possible; remove this cup from me; yet, not what I want, but what you want." The parts in Mark are (1) acknowledgment that for God all things are possible, (2) wish, and (3) surrender. As David Daube has pointed out, this is the four-part prayer of a pious Jew at the point of death minus the confession of sin.[11] For Jesus, whether he considered himself the Messiah or the Son of God, the omission of the confession of sin was to be expected. Mark is in the rabbinic tradition; Matthew and Luke have lost it. But that Mark was the original appears from a detail. Mark begins, "Father, for you all things are possible." Matthew begins, "Father, if it is possible." The fundamental acknowledgment has lost its point in Matthew, but the issue of possibility for God remains, although to little purpose.

But there is more. In Mark 14 Jesus had taken Peter, James, and

John along and told them to stay awake. The three slept. The rabbinic rule was that the Passover celebration was over when some of the company fell sound asleep.[12] So Jesus' admonition to the three to stay awake was pointed. In Luke 22.39ff. there is no such admonition, although we are told with little purpose at verse 45 that Jesus found the disciples sleeping.

My second example is Peter's denial of Jesus. David Daube has observed that a Jew, questioned by a Gentile, must not deny his Jewishness even at the risk of his life. Daube points out that the rabbis made two basic distinctions: first, between evasion and a direct no, and second, between a private and a public denial.[13] Evasion is less serious than a direct no. A private denial is not as bad as a public denial. This is precisely the pattern that is found in Mark 14.66ff. Peter was warming himself in the courtyard below when a servant girl of the high priest, looking at him, said, "You also were with Jesus of Nazareth" (Mark 14.67). Peter responded, "I neither know nor understand what you are saying" (14.68). The reply is a denial in private and an evasion. Peter went outside to the forecourt. The maid saw him again and said to bystanders, "This man is one of them" (14.69). Peter made the same denial (the Greek verb $\dot{\alpha}\rho\nu\acute{\epsilon}o\mu\alpha\iota$, to deny, is used in both verses), so again an evasion, but this time in public. After all, the maid made the accusation to bystanders. Subsequently, the bystanders said that he was surely one of them (14.70). Peter began to curse and swear, "I do not know the man of whom you speak" (14.71). This is a direct no, and it is made in public. Daube hesitates to claim that Mark is historically accurate. So would I, and I would rather feel that Mark has here a deliberate reminiscence of the rabbinic structure with a possible purpose. That possible purpose is to indicate to Christians that, if challenged by unbelievers, they should profess their faith.[14]

Peter's three denials of Jesus are also in Matthew, Luke, and John, so the denials clearly were very much part of the tradition. It is reasonable to believe that Matthew and Luke depend to some extent on their most important source, Mark. Luke shows no understanding of the rabbinic categories. A maid saw Peter as he sat by the fire among others (Luke 22.55f.). She said, "And this man was with him" (22.56). She spoke of Peter in the third person, so she was not addressing him but was speaking to the others. Peter denied it, saying: "I do not know him, woman" (22.57). So Peter's first denial is a direct no and is public. A little later another also said, "You are one of them" (22.58). We are not told that Peter had moved from the fire where others were. Peter replied, "Man, I am not" (22.58). So Peter's denial was again a direct no and presumably was public. About an hour later another said, "In truth this man was also with him, for he is a Galilean" (22.59). We are still not told Peter had moved from the fire. Peter said, "I don't know what you are saying" (22.60). Thus, in Luke, Peter's three denials are first two direct no's and a third evasion; the first certainly in public, the second and third presumably so. We may quickly note that in Matthew 26.69ff. all three denials are public: the first is an evasion and the second and third are direct no's; in John 18.25ff. all three denials are public and direct no's.

Still, in emphasizing the rabbinic structure in Mark as against Matthew when the episode is common to both, we must not overlook the rabbinic nature of the Sermon on the Mount, which does not occur in Mark. Two points stand out. First, in Matthew 5.2–10 we have the formulation "Blessed are *they*," but at the very end of this section we have a switch from the third person to the more immediate second person, "Blessed are *you*," and the circumstances for this are set out at greater length. This switch from third person to the direct second person address at the peroration with greater detail is from early rabbinic prayer.[15] Second, the famous antitheses in the sermon from verse 21 onwards, "You have heard . . .

but I say," is modeled on a form of rabbinic teaching. We are presented with an interpretation of Scripture that is then refuted by a better.[16] A comparison with the shorter version in Luke 6.20ff. will show how much of the rabbinic structure has been lost.[17]

The Sermon on the Mount in Matthew alerts us to a characteristic of the Gospels that will recur. The Gospels are composites with each evangelist drawing on a number of sources. This is particularly obvious for Matthew and Luke where both take from Mark and from a source common to Matthew and Luke but not to Mark and that is usually designated as Q, and where each also uses a source or sources not used by the other.[18] These sources will vary in their historical accuracy and plausibility. The structure of the Sermon on the Mount in Matthew is very rabbinic, but the structure in other parts of Matthew is less so. A conclusion to be drawn is that accuracy in one part of a gospel does not ensure accuracy in another.

Nothing that I have said in this introduction should be understood as implying that Mark's historicity or plausibility should be accepted without great caution. In the nature of things we should expect errors. Still, its faults are at times exaggerated. Traditionally Mark has not been held in the highest regard. One illuminating exaggerated criticism is by John P. Meier with regard to Mark's account of the execution of John the Baptist, which he says "contains little of historical worth."[19] He has two main arguments. First, the hostility of Herodias, Herod's wife, to John arose from his criticism of them because Herodias had been married to Herod's brother and thus their marriage was incestuous. But Herodias in Mark had been married to Herod's half-brother Philip (Mark 6.17) whereas Josephus who is to be preferred—I accept that Josephus is generally historically accurate—claims Herodias had been married to Herod, the son of Herod the Great.[20] But whether there is a contradiction is not easy to know. The family tree of Herod the Great's descendants is enormously complicated: he had ten wives.[21] It may well be that Philip and this younger Herod are one and the same.[22] But, in any event, the matter is of little consequence.[23] The author of Mark would have had little interest in exactly which brother had been the previous husband of Herodias. John's preaching against incest was valid in any case.

Meier's second argument seems at first to be stronger. John the Baptist was executed at Machaerus.[24] This, according to Mark 6.17ff., was during the dinner party where Salome was immediately given his head as she had requested. Machaerus is in Herod Antipas's second dominion, Peraea, yet Mark 6.21 says Herod Antipas gave the banquet for "his courtiers and officers and for the leaders of Galilee." No mention is made of the leaders of Peraea, so for Meier the feast appears to be held in Galilee, not Peraea. This is to ignore the fact that for the gospel writers Peraea as such was supremely unimportant. Certainly it was part of Herod Antipas's tetrarchy and was geographically separate from Galilee, but it was not considered a distinct entity by the gospel writers. Josephus certainly often terms it Πέραια,[25] but it is never called this in the New Testament except in variant readings in Luke 6.17. At Matthew 19.1 Jesus went away from Galilee and he entered the region of Judaea beyond the Jordan (πέραν τοῦ ιορδάνου). Mark would not list the leaders of Peraea specifically among the guests.

I would be inclined to see in this indifference to the political status of Peraea an issue that will surface again: the general lack of interest of Jesus and his followers as to the difference between the rule of the Romans and that of Herod Antipas. Galilee and Peraea were under Herod Antipas. Judaea was part of the Roman Empire. But the Gospels make Peraea out to be almost part of Judaea:

across the Jordan. Perhaps the authority of Herod Antipas and his Herodians was less apparent in Peraea.

Finally, I wish to stress how unimportant Jesus seemed outside Israel during his lifetime. Palestine was an insignificant part of the Roman Empire. For Rome Jesus is recorded only on account of the behavior of his followers after his death.

1

✛

"AND THE LARGE CROWD WAS LISTENING TO HIM WITH DELIGHT"

✛ ✛ ✛

I WISH TO BEGIN MY ACCOUNT OF THE LIFE OF JESUS WITH what appears an unremarkable text—indeed, with one sentence of it—but the sentence is pivotal. From it we will gain remarkable insights into Jesus' genealogy and birth, what he believed himself to be, and what others believed him to be. More important, the sentence is central to interpreting the differences between the Gospels, and its setting is of fundamental significance for understanding Mark and its structure. The sentence is in Mark 12.37: "And the large crowd was listening to him with delight." The episode to which the text relates (Mark 12.35ff.) occurs also in Matthew 22.41ff. and Luke 20.41ff., but there is no sign of the delight in these other two Gospels. What was the cause of the joy? If, as is generally accepted, Matthew and Luke were following Mark, why did they not report the joy? Modern commentators also often ignore the delight. Perhaps they have no explanation. Walter W. Wessel explains it rather weakly: "Mark goes on to say that the crowd was delighted to listen to Jesus. Apparently they enjoyed seeing the so-called experts stumped."[1] Indeed, the whole episode of which joy is the culmination presents problems for commentators, despite the obviously correct general explanation of the whole episode, which will be discussed shortly, having been given by David Daube.[2]

The immediate setting is Jesus' question, which he himself answers: "How can the scribes say that the Messiah is the son of David?" (Mark 12.35). But the question must be seen in the wider context of the four questions in Mark 12 that occur after the parable of the vineyard.

For the first of these questions Pharisees and Herodians come to trap Jesus (Mark 12.13ff.), and they ask him whether it is lawful to pay taxes to the Roman emperor. Next, "Sadducees who say there is no resurrection come to him" (12.18) and ask to whom at the resurrection a woman would be married who successively married seven brothers (12.18ff.).[3] This lead-in in Mark 12.18—they "come to him"—will turn out to be important for us: the Sadducees and the Pharisees do not pose their questions on the same occasion. Then a scribe who sees that Jesus answers well asks a third question (12.28): "What is the first commandment of all?" Finally, we have the fourth question, which most concerns us:

12.35. While Jesus was teaching in the temple, he said, "How can the scribes say that the Messiah is the son of David? 36. David himself, by the Holy Spirit, declared,
> 'The Lord said to my Lord,
> "Sit at my right hand,
> until I put your enemies under your feet." '

37. David himself calls him Lord; so how can he be his son?"
And the large crowd was listening to him with delight.

Again it is to be noticed that the question is put on a different occasion, this time while Jesus is teaching in the Temple. But on this
occasion the question is put not to Jesus but by Jesus, which is also
the testimony of Luke 20.41 and Matthew 22.41f.

The fourth question has caused commentators great difficulty.
For Vincent Taylor it "indicates, however obscurely, the mind of
Jesus on the question of Messiahship."[4] But he does not explain
how it does so. C. E. B. Cranfield, after noting that the question
seems to have been put by Jesus on his own initiative, goes on:
"But it seems unlikely that he would have done so; for he would
hardly have introduced it as a merely academic question, and that
he introduced it with a clear reference to himself is even more
unlikely. Moreover, it is most improbable that he would have
attacked a doctrine so firmly based on Scripture as that of the
Davidic descent of the Messiah."[5] C. S. Mann (who is aware of
Daube) correctly says that Jesus' question is usually seen as proof of
Jesus' Davidic descent, but, he says, it could as easily be interpreted
as casting doubt on the whole idea.[6] But in truth the incontrovert-
ible general solution—I do not see how it can be seriously contested—as to who posed the question was given by David Daube
in 1958–59.[7] From his solution it then becomes straightforward to
work out Jesus' meaning.[8]

The solution, as Daube shows, lies in the relationship of these
four questions to the Four Sons' section of the Passover Haggadah.
The clever son asks a question about law: the equivalent in Mark is
whether it is lawful to pay the Roman tax. Next, the wicked child
asks an improper question, usually about resurrection: equivalent
to the Sadducees' question about the widow and her seven hus-
bands. Then the simple child puts a pious question: equivalent to

the question of which is the first commandment. Finally, the fourth child cannot put a question and the father asks it: in Mark the fourth question is put not to Jesus but by Jesus.[9] The fourth Passover liturgical question is a question about contradictions: in Mark Jesus does question the very strong tradition that the Messiah would be the son of David. The parallelism is precise: in both Mark and the Haggadah there are four questions; the questions are all of different types, but the four types are identical in Mark and the liturgy; the types of question occur in the same order; the fourth question is put by the father or master, not by someone else as in the first three. A detail should be noted. In Mark, after the third question is answered we are told: "After that no one dared to ask him any question" (12.34). At the same point in the liturgy comes: "And with him who does not know how to ask you must open and begin yourself."[10] Coincidence cannot account for the parallelisms. Matthew 22.46, on the other hand, is so remote from the Passover ritual that it is after the fourth question that no one dares to ask Jesus again.[11]

If a relationship is undeniable, then the connection cannot be that the liturgy borrowed from Mark. How could the Passover liturgy derive from a heretical sect? Rather, the structure means that Mark borrowed from the Passover liturgy. As Daube has argued, it is inconceivable that the earliest Christians did not celebrate Passover, just as Jesus himself had done with his disciples.[12] In the tradition used by Mark, the questions of the four sons were on the traditional topics but were made to concern Jesus directly. It is immediately irrelevant but directly important in this connection that the evidence for the liturgy is later: the liturgy must predate Mark. It should be stressed that gaps in our information frequently make impossible the tracing of a development in practices.

The order of the four questions in other Jewish materials is different—further evidence of a dependence of Mark on the liturgy.[13]

This last point must be emphasized. It is often observed that the Jewish sources for law that exist are later than the lifetime of Jesus and hence cannot be relied upon as evidence for conditions in the early first century A.D. The observation is correct, but the conclusion is less secure. We must remember the enormous loss of source material. It may even happen, as in this instance, that the earliest record of Jewish practices or law is to be found in the New Testament.

The foregoing paragraphs entail that the structure of Mark, in this regard at least, is artificial. We thus have some confirmation of the evidence of Papias, bishop of Hieropolis around 130, recorded by Eusebius *Historia Ecclesiae* 3.39:

> The Elder used to say this also: Mark became the interpreter of Peter and he wrote down accurately, but not in order, as much as he (Peter) related of the sayings and doings of Christ. For he was not a hearer or a follower of the Lord, but afterwards, as I said, of Peter, who adapted his teachings to the needs of the moment and did not make an ordered exposition of the sayings of the Lord. And so Mark made no mistake when he thus wrote down some things as he related them; for he made it his special care to omit nothing of what he heard, and to make no false statement therein. . . . So then Matthew recorded the sayings in the Hebrew tongue, and each interpreted them to the best of his ability.

Mark has clearly tailored the four questions as Passover Eve questions. I noted earlier with some emphasis that the questions were not all put on the same occasion. Mark has undoubtedly manipulated the order of the questions for liturgical purposes,[14] whether he heard of the questions from Peter or not. As we saw, the arrangement of Peter's denial of Jesus in Mark also suggests that it was artificially created to make a point. And Papias tells us that

Mark is not in order. The question is how far other material in Mark has undergone a chronological change. The question will become important because in Mark there appears to be a continuing escalation of Jesus' hostility toward the Pharisees and eventually toward institutionalized Judaism.[15]

Matthew and Luke are instructive for the four questions. Matthew 22.15ff. follows the order of Mark. Luke 20.20ff has questions one, two, and four in the order of Mark, but not three. Question three is in a very different context (Luke 10.25ff.) and leads into the parable of the Good Samaritan, which appears only in Luke. We must presume that here as elsewhere Luke knew the Gospel of Mark and has chosen not to follow it. There are two serious possibilities that are not contradictory. First, Luke knew that Mark's order was unsatisfactory at least in part and Luke had another tradition that he followed. Second, he was unaware of the rabbinic tradition enshrined in Mark and for aesthetic reasons placed this question in a new setting. At any rate, Luke's treatment betrays some dissatisfaction with the arrangement of Mark.

The point of the fourth question and Jesus' reply in Matthew, Mark, and Luke is to indicate that the Messiah will not be a descendant of David. This, as we have seen, is an interpretation that has often been doubted. The doubt is not wholly surprising, because the argument attributed to Jesus is convoluted. Yet the interpretation is obviously the meaning of all three Gospels as we have them. The doubt comes not from the wording of the texts but from external considerations. The tradition was strong that the Messiah would be the descendant of David. How could Jesus deny this or even raise a doubt? What is his point?[16]

Jesus' purpose appears in Mark and only in Mark. For some time Jesus' teaching had attracted crowds, but only when he was approaching Jerusalem (11.8ff.) are we told that the people were enthusiastic: many spread their cloaks on the ground and spread leafy branches that they had cut in the fields and cried, "Hosanna!" But then shortly thereafter occurred the so-called cleansing of the Temple by Jesus (11.15ff.), which must have troubled many, inhibiting as it did the necessary Passover sacrifices and the payment of the Temple tax. Now Jesus declares in the Temple that the Messiah will not be the son of David: "And the large crowd was listening to him with delight." The people were waiting and hoping for the coming of the Messiah. They wanted to know what kind of a man Jesus was and the authority by which he acted as he did (11.28). The general expectation was that the Messiah would be a descendant of David: Jesus unexpectedly denies this, and they are delighted. He has removed an obstacle to their accepting him as the Messiah. Jesus in fact is implicitly revealing himself as the Messiah.

The people's joy is recorded in Mark but not in Matthew and Luke. In Matthew (1.1ff.) and Luke (3.23ff.) but not in Mark, Jesus' genealogy is traced to David. So joy on this account would be inappropriate in Matthew and Luke. A matter that must not be overlooked is that this question and its answer appear in all three Synoptic Gospels, but only in Mark does the answer have any purpose. In Matthew and Luke it is quite irrelevant and even troubling, since it contradicts the already contradictory Davidic descent that these Gospels give of Jesus through Joseph.

This irrelevance is instructive in at least three ways. First, why do the question and answer appear in Matthew and Luke at all? The explanation must be that they existed in the early tradition about Jesus, a tradition that was too strong to be ignored. But that leads to the second issue. The descent of Jesus from David must now be treated as suspect, a matter to be discussed in chapter 3. The third point is this very tradition that the Messiah would be descended from David. That seems to have been the strongest messianic tradition in the time of Jesus. It does not appear in Mark, because Jesus did not fit the mold. But it does reappear in the slightly later Matthew and Luke, because it was so firmly embedded in general belief, and Jesus is made to fit the mold. So at an early date the traditions about Jesus' birth and genealogy were being manipulated to meet expectations.

There is still more. At Acts 2.24ff. Peter says of Jesus:

"But God raised him up, having freed him from death, because it was impossible for him to be held in its power. 25. For David says concerning him,

'I saw the Lord always before me, for he is at my right
    hand so that I will not be shaken;
26. Therefore my heart was glad, and my tongue re-
    joiced; moreover my flesh will live in hope.
27. For you will not abandon my soul to Hades, or let
    your Holy One experience corruption.
28. You have made known to me the ways of life; you
    will make me full of gladness with your presence.'

29. Fellow Israelites, I may say to you confidently of our ancestor David that he both died and was buried, and his tomb is with us to this day. 30. Since he was a prophet, he knew that God had sworn with an oath to him that he would put one of his descendants on his throne. 31. Foreseeing this, David spoke of the resurrection of the Messiah, saying,

'He was not abandoned to Hades, nor did his flesh ex-
    perience corruption.'

32. This Jesus God raised up, and of that all of us are witnesses. 33. Being therefore exalted at the right hand of God, and having received from the Father the promise of the Holy Spirit, he has poured out this that you both see and hear. 34. For David did not ascend into the heavens, but he himself says,

'The Lord said to my Lord, "Sit at my right hand, 35.
    until I make your enemies your footstool."'
36. Therefore let the entire house of Israel know with cer-
tainty that God has made him both Lord and Messiah, this
Jesus whom you crucified."

So Mark uses a scriptural verse, Psalm 110.1, in a very complicated
way[17] as evidence that Jesus will be the Messiah yet not descended
from David. Matthew and Luke have the same verse but do not
use it apropos of Jesus as Messiah, though strangely and to no apparent purpose to claim that the Messiah will not be a descendant
of David. Now Acts uses the verse to prove that Jesus is both the
Messiah *and* the descendant of David. I accept the standard belief
that Luke and Acts had the same author, so the author contradicts
himself. The explanation, I believe, is as follows. Firmly fixed in
the overall tradition was the notion that this verse proved that Jesus
was the Messiah, hence it appears in that way in both Mark and
Acts. Also, because the argument from the verse was treated as
central, the verse appears in both Matthew and Luke. But there
was a problem. For many, including the redactors of Matthew and
Luke, the Messiah was to be descended from David, hence for
them the verse lost its point. Still, the belief continued that the
verse proved that Jesus was the Messiah. Hence it is so used again
later in Acts, but now it is reinterpreted to show Jesus was descended from David. Even at such an early date traditions on fundamental aspects of Jesus were fluid. The author of Luke-Acts used
two of them. To make the interpretation of Psalm 110.1 plausible
in Acts, it was removed from its context and no longer was quoted
by Jesus. There were those around Jesus who wanted him to be the
traditional Messiah.

I think we can go further. The tradition of the Psalm verse is in
all three Synoptics and in Acts. It is relevant, but with different

meanings, in Mark and Acts; it is irrelevant in Matthew and Luke. It is in both Luke and Acts, but the one redactor of these books used two different traditions. The verse in Mark and Acts is intended to show that Jesus is the Messiah. In all three Synoptics the verse is used in a very complicated way for the astonishing claim that the Messiah will not be descended from David. From this conglomeration of facts, especially the strange significance of Psalm 110.1, I believe it plausible to hold both that Jesus did in fact use this verse to indicate that the Messiah would not be descended from David and also that people took his use of it as evidence that Jesus himself was the Messiah.

If my arguments to this point are plausible, then two further implications are to be noticed. First, the crowd earlier did not believe or were unconvinced that Jesus was descended from David. For them this was a stumbling block to accepting Jesus as the Messiah. Second and more important, Jesus did not claim to be or even admit to being the Messiah. The crowd drew this conclusion. Why the reticence at this stage of his career? An explanation will be offered in chapters 9 and 10.

I wish to conclude the chapter in a very different way, discussing an issue that has already surfaced. If the evangelist Luke could use different strands of a tradition, then we must consider whether another evangelist could do the same. I have Mark specifically in mind because, as mentioned, I believe he is closest to the most accurate tradition. There is, I claim, a strong example in Mark 6.33ff. and Mark 8.1ff. concerning the feeding of the multitude. My argument derives from the conglomeration of similar features of the episodes coupled with significant differences.

The conglomeration of similarities are as follows:

(1) A crowd was around Jesus, it became late, they had nothing to eat, Jesus took responsibility for feeding them, and the only

food available was bread and fishes. In Mark 6 there were five loaves and two fish; in Mark 8 seven loaves and a few fish. The crowd, five thousand in Mark 6, four thousand in Mark 8, ate and were filled. Not only were they filled but in both accounts the leftovers were plentiful: twelve baskets of broken pieces and fish in Mark 6, seven baskets in Mark 8.

(2) The disciples then departed in a boat. In Mark 6 Jesus at first stayed behind, but in Mark 8 he went with the disciples.

(3) In the boat an issue about bread became important. In Mark 6 Jesus walked on water and the disciples were terrified, thinking he was a ghost; Jesus entered the boat and the wind stopped. The disciples were astonished, "for they did not understand about the loaves, but their hearts were hardened" (Mark 6.52). The reference to loaves is taken to refer to the feeding of the crowd, but there is no immediate connecting link in the text. The verse is understood by modern scholars in a theological way, but theology is usually remarkably absent from Mark. In Mark 8 the disciples had forgotten to bring bread and had only one loaf. Jesus told them to beware the yeast of the Pharisees and of Herod. "They said to one another, 'It is because we have no bread'" (8.16). Here the reference to bread has an immediate connection.

(4) In both Mark 6 and 8, the disciples do not understand, and this failure to understand is connected with bread.

(5) In both, the disciples' hearts were hardened (Mark 6.52; 8.17).

The connections are too close for coincidence, yet the episodes are related very differently. We cannot be dealing with two separate occasions. There is a mixing of a tradition. Both accounts cannot be true, neither may be accurate, and both may contain some elements of truth. But here again we have, in one gospel, two accounts of one episode from traditions that had diverged.

There is in Mark 4.35ff. a further episode that seems, though perhaps not so certainly, still another version of the same original tradition. This time there is no preceding miracle of loaves and fishes, but Jesus had been addressing a crowd (Mark 4.1ff.), although this time expressly in parables. As in Mark 8 he got into the boat with his disciples. As in Mark 6 the weather conditions were unfavorable. Jesus stilled the waves, controlling nature as he did when he walked on water in Mark 6. Again, as in both Mark 6 and 8, the disciples do not understand. But this time there is no feeding of the multitude, and no significance is given to bread.

What are we to make of these three accounts? At the very least, Jesus had addressed a large crowd, among whom there was considerable excitement. Then the disciples set sail in a boat, and an extraordinary event occurred. This was seen as so important that it was associated with a miracle. But the outstandingly significant feature of the tradition is that the disciples lacked faith and did not understand. The meaning of this must wait until chapter 11. (It will be noticed that if I am wrong and the three episodes are not to be treated as one, then the lack of faith and understanding on the part of the disciples is even more emphasized.) But the issue becomes fundamental when we observe that we do not know at this stage of the investigation what the lack of understanding and faith was all about. In Mark 4 the disciples did not understand that Jesus could control the wind and the sea. In Mark 6 they did not understand about the loaves; this is stressed even more than their terror when they thought Jesus was a ghost. In Mark 8 they are even more puzzled and relate Jesus' remark to the fact that they did not bring bread.

The evangelist Mark had one episode, but he recounted it in three different ways as if he had three different episodes. The episode must have been significant. But the traditions about it were deformed. We must be on our guard. When we have only one version of an event, the tradition there, too, may have been deformed. The significance of the episode, I will argue in chapter 11, is that the miracle was not of the kind that the disciples expected of Jesus, whom they thought was the Messiah who ought to be concerned with political matters.

2

✠

JOHN
THE
BAPTIST

✠ ✠ ✠

THE GOSPEL WRITERS WERE NOT WRITING HISTORY OR BIOGRAPHY. Other sources are sparse. Accordingly, to re-create the best tradition of the life of Jesus, one cannot always start at the beginning, as I hope I demonstrated in the previous chapter. But we must continue out of sequence. In chapter 5 I want to show that Jesus continually escalates his hostility to the Pharisees, but I must say here a few preliminary words on that subject for a different purpose. In Mark 1 we see Jesus believing he is beyond the law, but he acts with discretion and is not confrontational. In Mark 2 the Pharisees who are interested in him follow him around, and Jesus confronts them repeatedly. At the beginning of Mark 3 the Pharisees still watch Jesus, and he remains confrontational, acting against their cherished practices. Then, when he cures the withered hand on the Sabbath, we have this (Mark 3.6): "The Pharisees went out and immediately conspired with the Herodians against him, how to destroy him." From this point, the Pharisees have decided he is not like them and cannot be co-opted. But our interest in this chapter is not with the Pharisees but with the Herodians. The Herodians were not a recognizable religious group. They were simply the supporters of Herod Antipas, tetrarch of Galilee, where Jesus was. Why did they want him dead? The formulation "The A's then conspired with the B's to kill C" indicates that the A's have become hostile to C, but the B's were hostile to C even before. This is the first time the Herodians have surfaced in Mark, which confirms the interpretation. When we have a source that speaks repeatedly of the A's and never of the B's, and then suddenly says, "The A's conspired with the B's," then we know the source assumes that the hostility of the B's could be taken for granted by its hearers. But the Herodians' hostility must have been religious, not political. Jesus is never represented as having an overtly political stance. So why did the Herodians have their long-standing hostility? The answer lies in Jesus' connection with John the Baptist.

John was a historical person who appears not only in the Gospels but also in Josephus.[1] There are two versions of Herod's antipathy to him, which are sometimes thought to be mutually exclusive, sometimes reconcilable.[2] For me they come together to present a convincing picture. According to Mark 6.17ff., Herod imprisoned John and eventually had him beheaded. The immediate cause of the arrest according to Mark was that John criticized Herod because he had married his brother's wife, Herodias. In *Jewish Antiquities,* Josephus rather stresses political reasons:

18.116. But to some of the Jews the destruction of Herod's army seemed to be divine vengeance, and certainly a just vengeance, for his treatment of John, surnamed the Baptist. 117. For Herod had put him to death, though he was a good man and had exhorted the Jews to lead righteous lives, to practice justice toward their fellows and piety toward God, and so doing to join in baptism. In his view this was a necessary preliminary if baptism was to be acceptable to God. They must not employ it to gain pardon for whatever sins they committed, but as a consecration of the body implying that the soul was already thoroughly cleansed by right behavior. 118. When others too joined the crowds about him, because they were aroused to the highest degree by his sermons, Herod became alarmed. Eloquence that had so great an effect on mankind might lead to some form of sedition, for it looked as if they would be guided by John in everything that they did. Herod decided therefore that it would be much better to strike first and be rid of him before his work led to an uprising, than to wait for an upheaval, get involved in a difficult situation and see his mistake. 119. Though John, because of Herod's suspicions, was brought in chains to Machaerus, the stronghold that we have previously mentioned, and there put to death, yet the verdict of the Jews was that the destruction visited upon Herod's army was a vindication of John, since God saw fit to inflict such a blow on Herod.

The immediate question for us is why did some Jews view the destruction of Herod's army as God's vengeance for killing John. What is the connection? The war in question was in A.D. 36 with Aretas, king of Petra. Josephus tells us that Herod had long been married to Aretas's daughter. But Herod fell in love with Herodias, the wife of his half-brother. Herodias agreed to marry him when he returned from Rome whither he was bound, provided he first ousted his wife. His wife somehow found out this arrangement, asked him to send her to Machaerus, a fortress on the boundary of the lands of Aretas and Herod. Herod did so, unaware of his wife's knowledge of his intentions. The wife reached her father and told him what Herod was going to do. This was the cause of the war, although Josephus adds as an afterthought that Herod and Aretas also had a boundary dispute.[3] Jews considered Herod's defeat divine vengeance for his treatment of John. This opinion must be linked with the cause of the war, hence we have confirmation of Mark[4] that John was punished because he criticized Herod for marrying Herodias. John's stance is easily reconstructed. God at Leviticus 18.16 and 20.21 forbade sex, therefore forbade marriage (except for levirate marriage),[5] with a brother's wife. Herod married his half-brother's wife while his brother was still alive—indeed, Herod had gone to visit him.[6] John stood on God's word. When John called for repentance, he specifically singled out Herod as a sinner.[7] Josephus, in the passage quoted, stresses a political motivation for Herod: he feared that John's eloquence would cause a rebellion against him. The fear seems reasonable. In an important way Josephus confirms the accuracy of Mark.

John was known as "the Baptist." Nicknames are not given at random, so there was something special about the way he baptized. A ritual such as baptism or washing was common in ancient religions, and baptism was used to initiate a convert to Judaism.[8] But John was baptizing those who were already Jews. The meaning is that those who were born Jews or were converted were not really Jews until they received baptism from John. Josephus stresses that John used baptism not to forgive sin but to indicate that the soul was clean because of right behavior. The need for repentance was indeed the heart of John's message.[9] John was calling on Herod to repent and thus give up Herodias. It is no wonder that Mark can report: "And Herodias had a grudge against him, and wanted to kill him" (6.19).

The congruence of Josephus and Mark suggest we may have

some confidence in the reliability of Mark when he describes the Baptist. Some scholars believe that John was an Essene, but this seems contradicted by Mark 1.6 that John was dressed in camel's hair with a leather belt, whereas the Essenes dressed themselves in white.[10] John was clearly an ascetic[11] whose message of repentance was to Jews.[12] John foretold the coming of one more powerful than himself whose sandal he was not fit to untie (Mark 1.7). With the coming of this person the kingdom of God would come near. John certainly did not claim to be the Messiah.[13] Further precision of John's character and message is not needed here except that we should notice that he displays no hostility to the Romans, and he does not suggest that the great person who is coming will be the political Messiah who will drive out the Romans.

For the connection between John the Baptist and Jesus, we may leave to chapter 3 the implausible accounts of a blood relationship and take as a minimum the plainest account—in Mark—that actually gives all we need at this stage. All three Synoptic Gospels relate that John baptized Jesus.[14] To that extent and in some sense we must accept that at that point in time Jesus was a disciple of John. It does not necessarily follow that he so saw himself thereafter.[15] In Mark we are told nothing more about the relationship (although Jesus saw the heavens break open and the spirit descending, and heard a voice from heaven). We are not told in Mark that John knew who Jesus was or recognized him as the greater person who was to come after him. Luke 3.21 also does not record John recognizing who Jesus is. But in Matthew 3.13f. John is reluctant to baptize Jesus and indeed claims that it is he who needs to be baptized by Jesus. John's gospel has the Baptist proclaim that Jesus "is the Lamb of God who takes away the sin of the world" (1.29ff.). John does not actually state that the Baptist baptized Jesus, but I take that as the implication of the texts.[16]

Mark has this:

1.14. Now after John was arrested, Jesus came to Galilee, proclaiming the good news of God, 15. and saying, "The time is fulfilled, and the kingdom of God has come near; repent, and believe in the good news."

Thus, after John's arrest—but before his execution because that is not mentioned at this point—Jesus continued John's message of repentance but more strongly: the time was fulfilled and the kingdom of God was at hand.[17] Not only that, but Jesus had come into Galilee to proclaim his message. And Galilee was ruled by Herod Antipas. If Herod was afraid that the Baptist's ecstatic teaching of repentance could cause an insurrection, he would be equally afraid of Jesus even if Jesus did not name him as a sinner. In Galilee Jesus was drawing large crowds and performing miracles.[18]

Jesus may not even have left Herod alone. Mark 8.15 records that Jesus told his disciples to beware of the leaven of the Pharisees and of Herod; this is in the context of an argument with Pharisees, not with Herodians. People were asking, who is Jesus? Some said he was John the Baptist risen from the dead; others said he was Elijah or a prophet (Matthew 16.13; Mark 6.14ff., 8.27ff.; Luke 9.7ff.). The existence of the question and the answers is plausible. Jesus' connection with John the Baptist is enough to explain the hostility of the Herodians toward him (Mark 3.6) that seems earlier even than the hostility of the Pharisees. To explain Herodian hostility we do not have to accept that Herod himself believed Jesus was John the Baptist risen from the dead, even though for that we have the testimony of Mark 6.16 and Matthew 14.1f.

The connection—Herod, John the Baptist, Jesus—recurs in Matthew and Luke. In Matthew 14.13 Jesus withdrew by himself to a deserted place in a boat when he heard that Herod had executed John. At Luke 13.31 Pharisees came to Jesus and told him to flee because Herod wanted to kill him. At Luke 16.16 Jesus made the coming of John the turning point in the law and the prophets.[19]

In the circumstances it is plausible, whether true or not, that when the Pharisees wanted to trap Jesus with the question of whether it was lawful to pay taxes to the Romans they sent their disciples to him along with Herodians (Matthew 22.15ff.). The followers of Herod Antipas were natural allies of the Romans, and they had an antipathy to Jesus. One can also understand the existence of the tradition in Luke 23.6ff., implausible though it is,[20] that Pilate sent Jesus to Herod, with whom he was at enmity. The Herodian hostility toward Jesus for political reasons also played a role in the myth that Joseph and Mary fled to Egypt with the infant Jesus to avoid the massacre of the innocents by Herod the Great.

I stress this hostility of the Herodians toward Jesus because it adds a number of dimensions to our understanding. First, so far as we can tell from the surviving evidence, Jesus probably did not seek to provoke them as he did the Pharisees. The hostility resulted simply from the relationship that was believed to exist with John the Baptist. Second, throughout this hostility there is not the slightest indication in the sources that Jesus was interested in secular politics. Third, the Herodian involvement has so little to do with early Christianity or the denouement of Jesus' life that its survival in the Gospels is strong evidence of the continuing force of tradition. Fourth, the survival of this largely irrelevant Herodian hostility in the Gospels highlights the absence of any sign of hostility between Jesus and the Romans. That hostility did not exist, and that in turn should tell us much about Jesus' mission. It was not political.

Finally, the execution of John created a great sensation. The defeat of Herod Antipas by King Aretas, which Jews attributed to divine vengeance for Herod's execution of John, occurred in 36. But if we accept the traditional date of Jesus' execution as 30, then John's earlier beheading is to be dated to 29 or before, depending on the length of Jesus' ministry. So John's religious message was still very much alive eight years later and was politically dangerous. This itself is an indication that the Herodians would take any supposed connection between John and Jesus very seriously. Moreover, Josephus's account carries the clear implication that the Jews who believed that God punished Herod for beheading John were not the Christians. John has his own place in the history of religion, independently of Jesus.[21]

3
✠
JESUS
BEFORE
HIS
MINISTRY
✠ ✠ ✠

WE CAN NOW BEGIN TO EVALUATE THE STORIES SURROUNDING Jesus' birth.

To begin with we can discount the story of a blood relationship between Jesus and John the Baptist, which appears only in Luke (1.5ff.). In her old age, we are told, barren Elizabeth became pregnant by her husband, Zechariah. She was visited by her relative, Mary, who was also pregnant though a virgin (1.34), and Mary stayed with her about three months (1.56). Elizabeth gave birth to John (1.57ff.), and Mary to Jesus (2.5ff.). Despite the wondrous details, the story lacks conviction. The main argument is not that the tale does not appear in the other Gospels; after all, neither Mark nor John give any account of the birth of Jesus. The primary argument is that in Luke itself, when John was baptizing and proclaiming the coming of the Lord (3.1ff.), he seems not to have recognized Jesus. The sole texts in Luke on the baptism of Jesus read:

3.21. Now when all the people were baptized, and when Jesus also had been baptized and was praying, the heaven was opened. 22. and the Holy Spirit descended upon him in bodily form like a dove. And a voice came from heaven, "You are my Son, the Beloved; with you I am well pleased."

Nothing indicates that John saw the Holy Spirit descend upon Jesus. As if this were not enough, John's disciples subsequently reported Jesus' miracles to him.

7.18. The disciples of John reported all these things to him. So John summoned two of his disciples 19. and sent them to the Lord to ask, "Are you the one who is to come, or are we to wait for another?" 20. When the men had come to him, they said, "John the Baptist has sent us to you to ask, 'Are you the one who is to come, or are we to wait for another?'" 21. Jesus had just then cured many people of diseases, plagues, and evil spirits, and had given sight to many who were blind. 22. And he answered them, "Go and tell John what you have seen and heard: the blind receive their sight, the lame walk, the lepers are cleansed, the deaf hear, the dead are raised, the poor have good news brought to them. 23. And blessed is anyone who takes no offense at me."

John had taken so little interest in Jesus that Jesus' miracles had to be related to him by his own disciples. Even then John was not persuaded that Jesus was the person he was proclaiming.

The myth of blood relationship is a natural result of early Christian propaganda. As we saw in chapter 2 John remained famous, even popular, after his execution. He had proclaimed the coming of the Lord, and for the early Christians this was Jesus. Both John and Jesus (or at least Jesus' disciples) practiced baptism. Again, the hostility of the Herodians against Jesus because of John would also increase the feeling of a link between them. The tendency to exaggerate the link between John and Jesus recurs in a different way in John's account. There, although the world did not recognize Jesus (John 1.10), the Baptist knew who he was as soon as he saw him (1.29ff.), and he proclaimed him. He called him "the Lamb of God" (1.36), and two of his disciples actually left him and followed Jesus (1.37).

A second obvious myth is in Matthew 2: Herod the Great's slaughter of all the infants two years old or younger around Bethlehem because wise men from the East told him a child was born king of the Jews. This supposedly caused Joseph and Mary to flee Judaea to Egypt. I call it an obvious myth because there is no other evidence for the slaughter, which is inconceivable if the massacre existed, given that the ancient sources tell us a great deal about Herod.[1] This is so even if the number of infants around Bethlehem was not great. Still, some scholars are reluctant to dismiss it. Benedict T. Viviano claims, "Herod acts in character: the story may not be historical but possesses verisimilitude and is reminiscent of Pharaoh's command to kill the male offspring of the Israelites."[2] Much of the genesis of the myth can be traced. Herod was renowned for his unstable, excessive cruelty, and the Herodians—under Herod Antipas—were hostile to Jesus from the beginning of his ministry. The wise men term Jesus "the king of the Jews," a reminiscence of the inscription that Pilate placed on Jesus' cross: "Jesus of Nazareth, king of the Jews." The notion of the star that guided the wise men probably derives from a midrash on the story of Balaam, especially on Numbers 24.17:

> "I see him, but not now:
>> I behold him but not near—
> a star shall come out of Jacob,
>> and a scepter shall rise out of Israel:"

Here we have both the star and the scepter, the symbol of kingship arising from Israel. The flight to Egypt to safety is a parallel of the ancient Israelites' flight, recalled in Exodus. More detail is not needed.[3] The myth is to exalt Jesus, recognized as king of the Jews from birth, whose safety at birth is the parallel of the safety of all the Israelites.

At this stage a third early Christian myth can be set down: that Jesus was a descendant of David. First, the genealogies given in Matthew 1.1ff. and Luke 3.23ff., the only Gospels to treat the issue, are different. Second and more important, they cannot be seen as actually showing a line of descent from David.[4] Third and more important still, the Davidic descent of Jesus is traced in these Gospels through Joseph who, for their redactors, is emphatically not Jesus' father.[5] Fourth, that Jesus was a descendant of David is never again claimed in the Gospels. This is astonishing given the firmness of the tradition that the Messiah would be the son of David. Last and most important of all, we saw in chapter 1 that in all three Synoptics Jesus denied that the Messiah was descended from David. This is inexplicable given the tradition, unless Jesus was indirectly claiming or admitting to be the Messiah and getting around the particular difficulty that he was not descended from David.

But why do Matthew and Luke make Jesus out to be the descendant of David? The reason, I suggest, is that the tradition that the Messiah would be the descendant of David was so prevalent that this claim simply had to be made. But there were more versions of the Messiah than one. An issue that we will have to face in chapters 9 and 11 is whether Jesus' vision of himself as the Messiah—if he did so see himself—was the same as that of his early followers.

In Luke there is a further myth about the birth of Jesus.[6]

2.1. In those days a decree went out from Emperor Augustus that all the world should be registered. 2. This was the first registration and was taken while Quirinius was governor of Syria. 3. All went to their own towns to be registered. 4. Joseph also went from the town of Nazareth in Galilee to Judaea, to the city of David called Bethlehem, because he was descended from the house and family of David. 5. He went to be registered with Mary, to whom he was engaged and who was expecting a child. 6. While they were there, the time came for her to deliver her child. 7. And she gave birth to her firstborn son and wrapped him in bands of cloth, and laid him in a manger, because there was no place for them in the inn.

Quirinius is a historical figure mentioned by Josephus in *Jewish Antiquities:*

18.1. Quirinius, a Roman senator who had proceeded through all the magistracies to the consulship and a man who was extremely distinguished in other respects, arrived in Syria, dispatched by Caesar to be governor of the nation and to make an assessment of their property. 2. Coponius, a man of equestrian rank, was sent along with him to rule over the Jews with full authority. Quirinius also visited Judaea, which had been annexed to Syria, in order to make an assessment of the property of the Jews and to liquidate the estate of Archelaus. 3. Although the Jews were at first shocked to hear of the registration of property, they gradually condescended, yielding to the arguments of the high priest Joazar, the son of Boethus, to go no further in opposition. So those who were convinced by him declared, without shilly-shallying, the value of their property. 4. But a certain Judas, a Gaulanite from a city named Gamala, who had enlisted the aid of Saddok, a Pharisee, threw himself into the cause of rebellion. They said that the assessment carried with it a status amounting to downright slavery, no less, and appealed to the nation to make a bid for independence.[7]

Quirinius took a census when Judaea was incorporated into the Roman Empire. The purpose can only be taxation because Jews were exempt from service in the Roman army, since they would not fight on the Sabbath. So far Josephus agrees with Luke. But the census took place in A.D. 6 when Judaea was incorporated into the empire as part of the province of Syria. So Luke is wrong to place it in the reign of Herod the Great (Luke 1.5), who died in 4 B.C. Besides, in the time of Herod Judaea was not part of the Roman Empire, so it could not be taxed by Augustus. Nor did Augustus decree a census for the whole world, not even for the whole empire, but only for one province. This census is to be expected at a time of incorporation, as happened in A.D. 6. Nor could Augustus's decree extend to Joseph, who was a Galilean; at that time Galilee was not part of the empire but a client state ruled by the tetrarch Herod Antipas. Nor did Joseph own property in Bethlehem, or he would have had no difficulty in finding accommodation there. And a wife would not need to accompany her husband for registration on the census. A heavily pregnant Mary would not have gone with Joseph from Nazareth to Bethlehem, even if he himself had gone. The purpose of the myth is to show that the promise that the Messiah would be born in Bethlehem (Micah 5.2) was fulfilled in Jesus. But given the other manipulations of stories about Jesus' birth, we may doubt that he was born in Bethlehem.[8]

The truth would seem to be that the Evangelists had no reliable information about the birth of Jesus except that he was a Galilean of relatively humble parentage: his mother's name was Mary and her husband was called Joseph. Mark and John reasonably ignore the issue. Matthew and Luke record stories that presumably were current in their time but historically are impossible.[9] Presumably it would have been possible at a very early stage (Acts 1ff.) for Christians to have acquired knowledge of Jesus' life before his baptism by John, even from Mary herself (Acts 1.14). But that was not their concern.

As I have stressed from the outset, I believe that Mark represents the most accurate early tradition about Jesus.[10] But now I should emphasize that it is not this belief which persuades me of the implausibility of the accounts of Jesus' birth in Matthew and Luke. They are to be discarded because of their own internal impossibilities.[11]

I would like to emphasize that I am not suggesting bad faith on the part of the early Christians who created the myths. The myths would arise almost spontaneously to fill gaps in knowledge, providing their own dynamics. For example, it was widely held that the Messiah would be a descendant of David. Some of those who were fully convinced that Jesus was the Messiah would therefore believe that he must be descended from David. They would try to reconstruct his genealogy, but not all attempts would come out in the same way.[12]

4

JESUS AND JOHN THE BAPTIST

FOR JESUS, BAPTISM BY JOHN AND JOHN'S ARREST WERE BOTH cathartic. The Gospels of Mark and John both begin with John's preaching and his baptism of Jesus. In all three Synoptic Gospels, Jesus' baptism is immediately followed by his retreat into the desert. In all three, Jesus' ministry begins after John's arrest and seems conceptually linked. This need not indicate that Jesus remained a disciple of John after baptism, but some connection between Jesus' baptism by John, Jesus' going off into the wilderness, John's arrest, and Jesus' ministry is made plain. John's teaching was a catalyst, and when John had to stop, Jesus took over. It may be the case, although precision is not possible, that it was John's insistence that the Lord was at hand which caused Jesus to believe that he was that person.[1] Once again, the account in Mark is the most pointed and the most persuasive:

1.9. In those days Jesus came from Nazareth of Galilee and was baptized by John in the Jordan. 10. And just as he was coming up out of the water, he saw the heavens torn apart and the Spirit descending like a dove on him. 11. And a voice came from heaven, "You are my Son, the Beloved; with you I am well pleased."

When he was baptized Jesus saw the heavens open and the Spirit descending upon him. In Mark Jesus saw this, not John, not onlookers. That at least is what we are told. This version is repeated in Matthew, although in that gospel John had recognized Jesus' power before (Matthew 3.13ff.). In Luke the Holy Spirit descended upon Jesus in the bodily form of a dove (Luke 3.21f.), and we are not told who saw it. In John's gospel it is the Baptist who saw the Spirit descending upon Jesus (John 1.32).

A problem for some scholars is that the supposedly superior and sinless Jesus was baptized by the inferior John.[2] The explanation for me is that it was precisely baptism by John which caused Jesus to believe that he was the person prophesied by John.

Thus, in Mark, baptism made Jesus realize that *he* was the person of power proclaimed by John. He retreated to the desert for contemplation—there to be tempted, according to the Synoptics.[3] On John's arrest, he took up where John had been forced to stop, not as a follower of John but as the Lord. At first he showed discretion and did not confront the Pharisees, who were regarded as the most pious of the Jews. But, as we shall see in the next chapter, Jesus saw himself as beyond the law from the very beginning of his ministry.

Jesus' life before his baptism is scarcely known to us.[4] He was a village Galilean, possibly a carpenter (Mark 6.3). Beyond that we have nothing except that his mother was Mary. That is a fact that should no longer surprise. His baptism transformed him. In midlife Jesus began his ministry with the conviction that he was the Lord prophesied by John.

But who precisely did Jesus believe he was? At Mark 1.11 the Spirit addressed him as "my Son, the Beloved." At Mark 2.10 and apparently also at Mark 2.28 he calls himself the "Son of Man." Unclean spirits fell down before him and called him the "Son of God." At Mark 8.30 he admits to his disciples that he is the Messiah, and in the following verse he teaches them "that the Son of Man must undergo great suffering, and be rejected by the elders, the chief priests, and the scribes, and be killed, and after three days rise again." He refers to himself as the "Son of Man" again at Mark 8.38 and at 9.9, 9.12, 9.31, 10.33, and 10.45. Blind Bartimaeus addressed him as "Son of David" (10.47f.). At Mark 12.35ff. Jesus indirectly reveals himself as the Messiah. A long significant passage appears at Mark 13.3ff. Peter, James, John, and Andrew asked Jesus privately when the Temple would be destroyed. Jesus told them to be on their guard because many would come in his name and claim to be him. There would be false Messiahs (Mark 13.21f.), and Jesus here admits to being the true Messiah. After great desolation and suffering they would see the "Son of Man" coming with great power and glory (13.26). Jesus is obviously referring to himself. When Jesus tells his disciples one of them will betray him, he calls himself the "Son of Man" (14.21). At the point of his arrest Jesus says, "The Son of Man is betrayed into the hands of sinners" (14.41). At the high priest's question Jesus admits that he is the Messiah and then designates himself the "Son of Man" (14.62).

I have set out this catalog even though we are not yet at the stage to comprehend fully the precise significance of the terminology. In Mark Jesus' favorite term for himself is the "Son of Man," usually in the context of his suffering. Following his baptism he also appears to have considered himself the "Beloved Son" of God.

Only under direct questioning, first by disciples and then by the high priest, does he admit to being the Messiah. Otherwise he makes this admission only indirectly. I stress all this because Jesus may not have seen himself, or at least not primarily, as the Messiah. There were varying traditions about the Messiah, but he does not seem to have been thought to be the Son of God or someone who was to suffer.

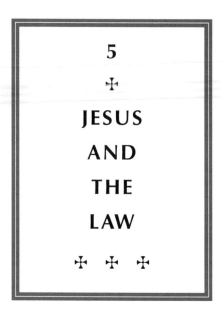

5

✠

JESUS
AND
THE
LAW

✠ ✠ ✠

IT SHOULD BE NO SURPRISE THAT TO UNDERSTAND JESUS'
ministry I begin with law. In Judaism divine law covered and cov-
ers all of life. Jesus' understanding and appreciation of law would
be fundamental for the attitude of others toward him. The Mishnah tractate Aboth is revealing. Two quotations from it will suffice.

> 3.19. R. Eleazar Hisma said: [The rules about] Bird-offerings
> and the onset of menstruation—these are essentials of the
> *Halakoth;* but the calculations of the equinoxes and gematria
> are but the savory dishes of wisdom.

Eleazar Hisma was active around the beginning of the second century. He is mentioned in Babylonian Talmud Horayot 10a as one
who could calculate the number of drops in the ocean. Herbert
Danby suggests that bird-offerings and the beginning of menstruation being difficult and complicated topics were to be accounted

the most important subjects of study.[1] Gematria is a cabalistic method of interpreting Scripture, but it may also mean geometry. I prefer to think that the message of Eleazar Hisma is that God is in every detail of daily life. In any event the text shows that details of the law were regarded as of great importance.[2] The same appears from Mishnah Aboth 4.2.

> Ben Azzai said: Run to fulfill the lightest duty even as the weightiest, and flee from transgression; for one duty draws another duty in its train, and one transgression draws another transgression in its train; for the reward of a duty [done] is a duty [to be done], and the reward of one transgression is [another] transgression.

Perhaps we should understand, "for the fulfillment of one duty draws the fulfillment of another in its train." The rabbis lived after the time of Jesus, but they continue the Pharisaic tradition, so we must examine Jesus' attitude toward the Pharisees.

Certainly, his behavior with regard to law is determined by other issues: Jesus' message, his beliefs about himself, and the response of the Pharisees. But if one takes Mark as presenting the best evidence for the historical Jesus (as I do), then one must start with Mark's remarkably clear portrayal.

The common dissatisfaction with Mark and my own stance are not paradoxical. If one is a Christian who fails to notice the strength of Mark's structure, one has a real problem. Why was the gospel written? What is the meaning for Mark of Jesus' message? Why does Jesus not overthrow the Romans? For the early tradition recorded by the evangelist, that presumably was to come. A later generation sought to resolve part of the problem by creating a new version of the Messiah.

What must not be overlooked in Mark is the progression in the episodes involving law. The episodes tend to occur in groups, with the group introducing a new stage. In Mark 1 as it now is—the chaptering is not original—there are four distinct episodes concerned with law, and they have interconnections. On the Sabbath Jesus cured a man possessed of an unclean spirit (Mark 1.21ff.). This he did in public. He did it by words alone and thus without breaching the prohibition against working on the Sabbath. Immediately thereafter, so still on the Sabbath, he cured Simon's mother-in-law by a laying on of hands (Mark 1.29ff.). Thus, he breached the prohibition on Sabbath working.[3] But this he did in private, inside a house in the presence only of his disciples. "When evening came, after sunset," people brought their sick to be cured (Mark 1.32). The repetition only in Mark[4]—evening had come and the sun had set—emphasizes that the Sabbath had ended. So although the people had seen him cure without working, the idea of respect for the Sabbath is depicted as so strong that people waited until it ended before they approached him.[5] Later in the chapter he cured the leper by a laying on of hands (Mark 1.40ff.). Thus, he made himself unclean (a necessary deduction from Leviticus 13.45f.): this was unnecessary because we have already been shown that his words were sufficient. This laying on of hands was in private; otherwise, he would not have commanded the leper to tell no one. Still, he also told the leper to show himself to the priest and make the offerings commanded by Moses.[6]

The episodes contrast public and private healings: in fact, the order is public, private, public, private. In the private healings Mark shows Jesus as regarding himself as beyond the law: he worked on the Sabbath, he made himself unclean. But Mark also shows Jesus as far from confrontational. In the first public healing, on a Sabbath Jesus cured without working: in the second it is emphasized that the Sabbath was over. Again, although Jesus made himself unnecessarily unclean, he ordered the cured leper to tell no one and to follow the law.

These four legal episodes all concern a miracle, specifically of healing. They recur in Matthew to some extent (8.14ff., 8.2ff.) and in Luke (4.33ff., 4.38ff., 5.12ff.), but the structure is lost and they are not placed at the outset of Jesus' ministry, as they are in Mark.

In what now appears as chapter 2, Mark takes us to a new stage. There are again four episodes—four is not significant—involving law, and they are treated as a unit. They have a fivefold common structure. 1. Jesus or his disciples behave in a surprising way. 2. This prompts a question from Pharisees or scribes. 3. Jesus replies in a way that silences the questioners. 4. The Pharisees or scribes are not represented as obviously being hostile. 5. Each episode concerns a specific event.

In one respect the first episode, the healing of the paralytic, in chapter 2 is transitional. Like all four episodes in chapter 1, it involves a miracle whereas none of the other three in chapter 2 does. Still, it differs in a most significant way from those in chapter 1. Jesus is shown as confrontational. This is Jesus' first brush with authorities, and it was he, not they, who brought it on (Mark 2.1ff.). Jesus said to the paralytic, "Your sins are forgiven," words which had to be offensive as they implied that the speaker knew God's mind. Scribes who were present thought but, significantly for Mark, did not say that Jesus was "blaspheming." Jesus rounded on them. The scribes were not seeking to trap him. And Jesus used an argument that would not satisfy them. He asked rhetorically whether it was easier to say, "Your sins are forgiven" or "Take up your mat and go home." But that was not the issue. The issue was the offensiveness of Jesus' first verbal formulation. He then went even further and insisted that the Son of Man—himself—had authority to forgive sin (Mark 2.10f.).

This episode is also in Matthew and Luke but with vital variations that show the power of Mark. In Matthew the scribes *said* to themselves, "This man is blaspheming" (9.3), but Jesus perceived their *thoughts* (9.4). Luke 5.17ff. is to the same effect. Matthew and Luke follow Mark but fail to make Jesus quite so confrontational.

The other three episodes in Mark 2 have further elements in common that distinguish them from the first: in all three the question is expressed and, perhaps strangely, it is not addressed to the actor. The second episode was Jesus' eating with tax collectors and sinners (Mark 2.15ff.), which was considered improper for the pious.[7] The scribes of the Pharisees asked his disciples why *he* did so, a question not necessarily hostile but seeking his motivation. Jesus' reply was again confrontational. His response, "I have come to call not the righteous but sinners," implies that he had no business with Pharisees, who are thus excluded from his mission.

The third episode involves the question to Jesus why *his disciples* did not fast (Mark 2.18ff.). Fasting twice a week had become a mark of piety but was not obligatory.[8]

The fourth episode (Mark 2.23ff.) has the Pharisees ask Jesus why *his disciples* plucked grain—worked—on the Sabbath, which was unlawful. Jesus' reply was not to the point and would not be persuasive to the Pharisees. Scripture (Exodus 16.25f.) forbade reaping on the Sabbath, and by interpretation plucking grain was reaping.[9] The rule being based on scriptural law was thus *halakah.* Jesus' legalistic response was that there was a precedent: David and his companions ate the consecrated bread. This behavior was not a rule, however, but an example, a matter of religious importance that did not affect the law. It was thus *haggadah,* which could not prevail over *halakah.* Besides, the precedent was not in point: it did not concern a breach of the Sabbath. And what was permitted to David need not have been permitted to others.

This second group of four episodes differs in other ways from the first group. They all have Jesus using language that indicates he believed he was someone very special. More important, they now have the Pharisees following Jesus to discover what kind of a person he was.

The legal episode at the beginning of Mark 3, the curing of the withered hand on the Sabbath, marks an ending and a beginning. It is connected with the episodes in Mark 2: the Pharisees were still watching Jesus, Jesus was still the one who began the confrontation, and he again used an inappropriate argument about law. But the episode marks a new phase: the Pharisees watched him *with hostility,* and then they plotted (with the Herodians) to kill him. They had decided he was not like them and could not be co-opted. Since he used inappropriate arguments about law of religious importance, he also could not be the Messiah.

Jesus was being watched to see whether he would cure a withered hand on the Sabbath. He asked, "Is it lawful to do good or harm on the Sabbath, to save life or to kill?" The question was palpably unfair. There was no prohibition on doing good on the Sabbath, only on working. Even more to the point, for the Pharisees it was lawful to work on the Sabbath in order to save life.[10] Jesus shows not only indifference to and ignorance of rabbinic law but also contempt for the Pharisees.[11]

The other episode in this chapter is relevant for the tightness of Mark's structure and his understanding of law in a different way (Mark 3.21ff.). People were saying that Jesus had gone mad, and his family came to restrain him, as was proper under Jewish law. When he was told that his mother, brothers, and sisters were looking for him, he neatly replied, "Whoever does the will of God is my brother, sister, and mother." He thus denied that his blood relatives had legal authority over him. The legal point that gives the episode its meaning is lost in Matthew 12.46ff.[12]

There are two episodes with legal implications in Mark 5, and surprisingly they are intertwined (as they also are in Matthew

9.18ff. and Luke 8.40ff.). Such intertwining of episodes occurs nowhere else in the Gospels.

Jairus, a leader of the synagogue, begged Jesus to lay hands on his little daughter, who was at the point of death (Mark 5.23). Jesus went with him, and a large crowd followed (5.24ff.). Now the second episode intrudes. A woman who had been hemorrhaging for twelve years touched his robe, believing that if she did so she would be healed. She was cured, and when Jesus asked who had touched him, she told him *the whole truth* "in fear and trembling." Then Mark reverts to Jairus's daughter. Before Jesus reached the house, he was told she was dead (5.35). Inside, he claimed she was only asleep, told her to rise, touched her, and she did rise (5.39ff.).

What these episodes have in common is that Jesus is rendered unclean by contact with a woman. For the structure of Mark we should notice that there is again a marked escalation. The hemorrhaging woman, by touching Jesus, made him unclean according to Scripture (Leviticus 15.19ff., esp. 15.25), and this uncleanliness lasted until evening (15.19). That is why the woman was terrified by what she had done—a point not noted in Matthew, although it is in Luke (8.47). By touching the dead girl, Jesus made himself unclean for seven days (Numbers 19.11). The escalation is not just that in the second episode the period of uncleanliness is longer. It is also that in the first it was the woman who made Jesus unclean, whereas in the second it was Jesus who made himself unclean. But the fact of uncleanliness is not mentioned for either episode. Mark, by intertwining the stories, is making the point that Jesus was unconcerned about ritual purity. It must be emphasized that the importance of ritual purity was established expressly by God, not by Pharisaic interpretation.

That Jesus, when he raised Jairus's daughter, made himself unclean is further emphasized by what is not set out. Jesus said, "The child is not dead but sleeping" (Mark 5.39). If she were only asleep, then touching her would not render him unclean. But Jesus' declaration was treated with ridicule. Mark 5.40 records that those present laughed at Jesus. After the event, "they were overcome by amazement" (5.42). Even more significant, Jesus then "strictly ordered them that no one should know this" (5.43). Why would he do this if he had simply awakened a girl from sleep?

At the beginning of Mark 7 Jesus is asked by the Pharisees and scribes why, contrary to tradition, his disciples ate without washing their hands. Jesus took this as an opportunity to attack the Pharisees quite unjustifiably. He accused them of abandoning the commandment of God and holding to human tradition (Mark 7.6ff.). He illustrated with a contrast between God's command to honor father and mother on the one hand and Corban—improperly understood as an offering to God—on the other, which would deny its use for parental support.[13] But the strictness of the necessity for keeping an oath was not enjoined by Pharisaic tradition but by a commandment of God set out in Deuteronomy 23.21ff., Leviticus 27, and Numbers 30.2. In fact, the Pharisees actually tempered the inviolability of oaths (Mishnah Nedarim 2.3). We should note in passing that for the Pharisees there would be no difference between Scripture and their interpretation of it.[14]

Subsequently (Mark 7.14ff.) Jesus declared that food does not make one unclean. The pronouncement was made with an absence of clarity, and only privately did he expand on his meaning to the disciples. Jesus thus again apparently pronounced against the express commandment of God in Leviticus, but a different explanation is offered in my next chapter.

At Mark 10.2ff. Jesus in effect condemned divorce, although Moses allowed it (Deuteronomy 24.1ff.). It is sometimes claimed by modern scholars that Jesus was not changing the law: after all, the argument goes, Moses did not command divorce.[15] The argument is false. There is a vast legal difference between a system that permits divorce and one that forbids it. To divorce I will return. Still, Jesus' prohibition of divorce is best seen as a moral commandment rather than a legal abrogation.[16]

The so-called cleansing of the Temple is told in Mark 11.15ff. in a way that is much more muted than in John 2.13ff. But Jesus' atrocity toward Pharisees, Sadducees, and all observing Jews alike shines through. Jesus threw out those buying and selling in the Temple, that is, in the Temple precincts (Mark 11.15).[17] But the sales, as we know from John (2.14ff.), were of the sacrificial animals: cattle, sheep, and doves. The sale of such was permitted in the Temple by the Temple authorities—indeed, the sale of doves was directly under their control (Mishnah Shekalim 6.5). Only religiously clean animals could be offered for sacrifice, and apart from sales in the Temple precincts these would not be easy to find, especially by pilgrims coming to Jerusalem for the festival. God, moreover, had centralized worship, and sacrifice could be offered only in one place, Jerusalem (Deuteronomy 12:16.5f.). Thus, Jesus was inhibiting the necessary sacrifices to God, at the one place where they were permitted and, at that, just before Passover, the holiest day of the Jewish year. Jesus was not only protesting abuses by the sellers. He also drove out the buyers (Mark 11.15), those who had come to offer pious sacrifice.

Jesus then overturned the tables of the money changers. Their function was religious or quasi-religious: to enable the Temple tax to be paid. Roman denarii with the portrait of Tiberius on the obverse, and the graven image of a false deity—Pax in the form of Tiberius's mother, Livia—on the reverse could not be offered. Similar objections applied to Greek didrachms. The money changers gave unobjectionable Tyrian coinage in exchange. So Jesus was preventing the payment of the Temple tax.[18]

Such are the passages in Mark that relate to Jesus and the law that is set out in Leviticus and Deuteronomy. It must be stressed that Jesus' hostility is not just to Pharisaical interpretation but to the laws of God themselves. There are six observable stages in Jesus' behavior. At stage one, Jesus thinks he is beyond the law, but he behaves with discretion and does not disclose the fact. At stage two, Jesus is confrontational, and the Pharisees follow him about to find out what kind of a person he is. At stage three, Jesus is even more confrontational, and the Pharisees become hostile. At stage four Jesus displays open indifference to ritual purity. At stage five Jesus becomes still more confrontational, attacking the Pharisees verbally. At stage six Jesus is physically violent in obstructing the Passover sacrifice and payment of the Temple tax.

Something very odd is going on. The legal passages relate to Jesus' hostility to the prohibition of working on the Sabbath, to laws of purification, to dietary restrictions, to sacrifice in the Temple, and to the payment of the Temple tax. In effect, they concern those matters which in the annual round of life show a Jew that he is a Jew. But this hostility cannot be because Jesus wanted to assimilate Jew and Gentile. In Mark Jesus' mission is decidedly not to the Gentile.[19] Although Mark ignores that issue, the Gospel's stance is obvious from Jesus' reaction to the Syrophoenician woman who wanted her daughter cured (7.24ff.). The symbolism is obvious: the children are the Jews, and the dogs are the Gentiles.

But what about the laws in Leviticus that have a moral content? They are almost ignored by Mark's Jesus, except for divorce. Jesus not only forbade divorce. He declared, "Whoever divorces his wife and marries another commits adultery against her, and if she divorces her husband and marries another, she commits adultery" (Mark 10.11f.). So Jesus was presumably in favor of the seventh commandment, which forbade adultery. But Jesus' whole treatment of the issue is strange.[20] There is also the blanket condemnation of evil coming from within.

Mark 7.20. And he said, "It is what comes out of a person that defiles. 21. For it is from within, from the human heart, that evil intentions come: fornication, theft, murder, 22. adultery, avarice, wickedness, deceit, licentiousness, envy, slander, pride, folly. 23. All these evil things come from within, and they defile a person."

But this is unspecific and does not take us very far. Who would not declare that such conduct defiles? And even this much he explained only privately to his disciples.

But otherwise in Mark there is nothing about Jesus' attitude toward God's laws in Leviticus that might be regarded as having a moral content, such as laws against incest (Leviticus 18.6ff.), sacrificing offspring to Molech (18.21), male homosexuality (18.22), bestiality (18.23), theft, fraud, and lying (19.11,13), harsh dealings with poor employees and the deaf and the blind (19.13f.), laws to benefit the poor (19.9f.), and so on. This cries out for an explanation.

Likewise unspecific but of great moral significance is Mark 12.28ff.:

One of the scribes came near and heard them disputing with one another, and seeing that he answered them well, he asked him, "Which commandment is the first of all?" 29. Jesus answered, "The first is, 'Hear, O Israel: the Lord our God, the Lord is one; 30. you shall love the Lord your God with all your heart, and with all your soul, and with all your mind, and with all your strength.' 31. The second is this, 'You shall love your neighbor as yourself.' There is no other commandment greater than these."

Mark's Jesus has no precise moral, social, or spiritual message except for any that is inherent in his miracle cures. But these miracle cures may have had a different function, such as to demonstrate his powers or to show that he was the Messiah. At the very least, as we shall see, one should say there is no emphasis in Mark on a specific spiritual message from Jesus.

But then why the stress on Jesus' opposition to those commandments of God that had no obvious ethical content? The only explanation that seems plausible to me is that Jesus as the charismatic religious leader believed from the beginning of his mission that he was above or beyond these laws, that when he recognized his inevitable opposition to the institutional religious leaders, the Pharisees, he set himself up to confront them, becoming more and more hostile. Eventually, in the cleansing of the Temple he also roused the anger of the Sadducees and brought about his own death (deliberately, I think).

Why was Mark written at all, with a Jesus hostile to those laws specific to Jews, and with no emphasis on an ethical or spiritual message? The answer for me is that the author accepted the Resurrection as a proven fact, from which it followed for him that Jesus was the Messiah. Nothing else was of consequence.

One final issue should be addressed. There is a marked difference in the hostility to Jesus in the Gospels and to his earliest followers in the first chapters of Acts. In the Gospels the hostility comes from the Pharisees until near the end when the Sadducees are brought in on account of the cleansing of the Temple. At the beginning of Acts, the Sadducees are the enemies of the early disciples.

4.1. While Peter and John were speaking to the people, the priests, the captain of the temple, and the Sadducees came to them, 2. much annoyed because they were teaching the people and proclaiming that in Jesus there is the resurrection of the dead. 3. So they arrested them and put them in custody until the next day, for it was already evening.

Peter and John were released.

5.17. Then the high priest took action; he and all who were with him (that is, the sect of the Sadducees), being filled with jealousy, 18. arrested the apostles and put them in the public prison.

When the Sanhedrin wanted to kill Peter and John it was Gamaliel, a Pharisee, who successfully spoke up in their defense (Acts 5.33ff.). The hostility of the Sadducees to these disciples is self-explanatory on one level. They did not believe in resurrection, but the disciples were giving Jesus as an actual example: one who was, moreover, the Messiah. The Sadducees might not live in continual enmity with the Pharisees, who believed in resurrection—why should they care overmuch about others' beliefs?—but the claims of the disciples were in different case, giving Jesus as real proof that the Sadducees were wrong. More surprising is that the Pharisees, who were zealous against Jesus, were much less hostile to the disciples. In fact, I should like to stress that even during Jesus' lifetime Pharisaic hostility to the disciples was muted. Even when the disciples plucked grain on the Sabbath—wrongfully in the eyes of the Pharisees—it was Jesus they questioned, not his disciples (Mark 2.23ff.).

Nor can the Pharisaic opposition to Jesus be attributed to his basic call for repentance. Rather, it is Jesus' opposition to the law as the Pharisees perceived it that really angered them. He set himself up in opposition to the Pharisees. The disciples were more restrained and did not offer a challenge—indeed, they often failed to understand Jesus—and were ignored.

Evidence for the argument in the preceding paragraph is again to be found in the early chapters of Acts. Until the appearance of Stephen, Jesus' followers are not shown as breaching prohibitions against working on the Sabbath, eating food declared unclean by God, ignoring female ritual uncleanliness, wantonly making themselves unclean by unnecessary contact with a corpse or leper, or failing to wash their hands before eating. In fact, they are not represented as acting against the Pharisaic view of the law.[21] So far were the disciples removed from law-breaking after Jesus' death that Peter is represented as not knowing that food previously declared unclean could be eaten (Acts 10.9ff.). So puzzling was this to him that he interpreted it as meaning he could carry Jesus' message to the Gentiles. Matters change with the advent of Stephen, who was believed to claim Jesus would destroy the Temple and change the law of Moses (Acts 6.8ff., esp. v.14). "They stirred up the people as well as the elders and the scribes" (Acts 6.12); so the Pharisees were at enmity with Stephen as previously with Jesus. Stephen was lynched and became the first Christian martyr. Stephen may have been alone among the early Christians in claiming that Jesus would destroy the Temple and change the law of Moses.[22] Saul approved of the killing of Stephen (Acts 8.1), and Saul was a Pharisee.[23]

We have the beginnings of an apparent paradox. Mark portrays Jesus as an opponent of the law, especially as seen by the Pharisees. Mark does not portray the disciples during Jesus' lifetime in the same way. Nor do the early chapters of Acts show the first disciples as hostile to the law after Jesus' death. What in Mark is of great importance in the portrayal of Jesus is represented as of no significance for his disciples during his lifetime and immediately thereafter. Whatever Jesus is about, his disciples show no understanding. The wider failure to understand on the part of the disciples is treated in chapter 11.

6

✠

MARK 7.19:
DID JESUS
DECLARE
ALL FOOD
CLEAN?

✠   ✠   ✠

A PIVOTAL ISSUE AND ONE THAT HAS GREATLY TROUBLED
scholars is whether Jesus declared all food clean. If he did, then in
this regard he went further in opposing God's commands than he
ever did elsewhere.

Jesus is recorded in Mark 7.17ff. as explaining a parable in private to his disciples. The latter part of Mark 7.19—as it usually appears in translations—is often treated as the evangelist's own explanation: "Thus he declared all food clean." But scholars note the
problems. First, if for Jesus no food was unclean, then he was
preaching in flat contradiction to God's commandments on clean
and unclean food in Leviticus 11. Not only that, but God's commandment was expressed in strong language: the food is "detest-
able" or "abominable" (11.10ff.) Moreover, as E. P. Sanders has

stressed, Scripture contains no provision for making unclean food clean, and no purification rite exists to make clean the person who eats unclean food. It should be noted, too, that in Scripture food prohibitions differ from laws of Sabbath observance in that the former are spelled out in detail whereas the latter are not.[1] Jesus could not claim that he was following the law of God but denouncing Pharisaic interpretation.

Second, nowhere else does Jesus pronounce against God's law as set out in Scripture. Jesus' pronouncements against divorce are a different case. There he acknowledges, as he does not here, that he is advocating a different standard. Again, there he justifies his stance: Moses allowed divorce because of the "hardness of your heart."[2] Finally, to judge from Matthew 19.9 Jesus did not prohibit divorce, even for cause, as a matter of law.[3] His words "Anyone who does divorce" implies that divorce is still possible, although it is immoral. It is, thus, no surprise that a scholar such as E. P. Sanders can hold that the words in Mark 7.15 (understood as claiming that all food is clean) appear "to be too revolutionary to have been said by Jesus himself."[4]

Third, the reason for any such ruling on food by Jesus is not at all clear. Jesus' pronouncement to the crowd is not made in order to enhance loving kindness. The abrogation of dietary restrictions is in no way in the interests of a higher morality. Addressing the crowd, Jesus does not even speak to the moral issue. The teaching that what comes out of a person's heart such as fornication or murder defiles is made to the disciples alone, and it is not logically dependent on any claim that no food defiles.

Fourth, and related to the above two points, there is no precedent for this. It is instructive to contrast Jesus' so-called cleansing of the Temple. The point of Jesus' action there is disputed, but that need not detain us here. What matters is that there was a precedent of hostility to the Temple. I would relate Jesus' behavior to Isaiah's teaching that God did not want sacrifice in the absence of repentance (see chapter 12).

Daniel J. Harrington very properly asks, "If the saying were so clearly Jesus' teaching on the Jewish food laws, why did no one use it in the debate about the obligation of Gentile Christians to observe the food laws?" He also asks, "If Jesus had been so explicit about the observance of Jewish food laws, why were there so many debates on this matter in the early church?"[5]

Finally, if Jesus had declared all food clean (and had been understood), his revolutionary teaching would have caused a sensation. But of that there is no sign. Still, despite the foregoing, most scholars accept that Jesus did declare all food clean.[6] C. S. Mann, for instance, claims that the saying "bears all the marks of being genuine, since such a sentiment would not have been common in contemporary Judaism."[7] In the past I accepted the majority view mainly because of Acts 10.9ff., which is often understood in the contrary sense:

> About noon the next day, as they were on their journey and approaching the city, Peter went up on the roof to pray. 10. He became hungry and wanted something to eat; and while it was being prepared, he fell into a trance. 11. He saw the heaven opened and something like a large sheet coming down, being lowered to the ground by its four corners. 12. In it were all kinds of four-footed creatures and reptiles and birds of the air. 13. Then he heard a voice saying, "Get up, Peter; kill and eat." 14. But Peter said, "By no means, Lord; for I have never eaten anything that is profane or unclean." 15. The voice said to him again, a second time, "What God has made clean, you must not call profane." 16. This happened three times, and the thing was suddenly taken up to heaven.

Some claim that it would be surprising if Peter had to be reminded that God had declared all food to be clean.[8] This fails to convince. After all, Jesus had not commanded the eating of all kinds of food, and in the Israel of his day, some prohibited species such as pigs might not have been readily available, and others such as birds of prey and snakes would have been thought unappetizing. A disciple might well need to be reminded. The argument from the text that persuaded me that Jesus declared all food clean is that Peter would not have had the authority on his own to make such a claim, and we know of no other source.

I now believe Jesus made no claim that all food is clean. My primary reason is that it is so out of keeping with the rest of his teaching, even including his opposition to the Pharisaic interpretation of the law.[9] Still, an explanation must be found for Mark 7.14ff., especially verse 19, and for Acts 10.9ff. My explanation begins with my claim that Jesus did say something akin to what is attributed to him in Mark 7.14ff. but that his meaning was different:

> Then he called the crowd again and said to them, "Listen to me, all of you, and understand: 15. there is nothing outside a person that by going in can defile, but the things that come out are what defile."
>
> 17. When he had left the crowd and entered the house, his disciples asked him about the parable. 18. He said to them, "Then do you also fail to understand? Do you not see that whatever goes into a person from outside cannot defile, 19. since it enters, not the heart but the stomach, and goes out into the sewer?" (Thus he declared all foods clean.) 20. And he said, "It is what comes out of a person that defiles. 21. For it is from within, from the human heart, that evil intentions come: fornication, theft, murder, 22. adultery, avarice, wickedness, deceit, licentiousness, envy, slander, pride, folly. 23.

All the evil things come from within, and they defile a person."

My suggestion is that Jesus did mean that food considered unclean was clean. But he was not declaring that food of a species that God declared unclean was clean. Rather, his point was that food of a species considered clean did not become unclean by contamination. That is to say that he was once again attacking Pharisaic interpretation of Scripture. He expressed himself as he did because he was quite unaware that anyone could subsequently misunderstand him and think that he was declaring God's prohibited food clean.

In what follows I wish to establish two things. First, I want to indicate something of the scope of Pharisaic interpretation on food that was not prohibited becoming unclean. Second, I want to establish that Jesus was concerned with denying validity to that interpretation.

There should be no doubt that, in the time of Jesus, types of food not proscribed by God were subject to becoming unclean in the sense that their consumption defiled the consumer. The main source of evidence is the Mishnah, where the subject of uncleanliness is prevalent. A few examples will be sufficient.

> Mishnah Kelim 1.1. These Fathers of Uncleanness, [namely,] a [dead] creeping thing, male semen, he that has contracted uncleanness from a corpse, a leper in his days of reckoning, and Sin-offering water too little in quantity to be sprinkled, convey uncleanness to men and vessels by contact and to earthenware vessels by [presence within their] air-space; but they do not convey uncleanness by carrying.

Fathers of uncleanliness is a term that refers to persons or things that are capable of conferring uncleanliness on other persons or things.

The importance of the text here is that an unclean earthenware vessel renders its contents unclean, and they in turn defile a consumer. These vessels are so subject to uncleanliness that the "father of uncleanliness" does not need to touch the vessel: it is enough if it is within its airspace.

> Mishnah Kelim 7.5. If a cock swallowed a creeping thing and fell within the air-space of an oven, the oven remains clean; but if the cock died there, the oven becomes unclean. If a creeping thing was found in an oven, the bread in it suffers second-grade uncleanness because of the oven's first-grade uncleanness.

This text indicates the subtlety and detail of the learning. Our main interest is in the second sentence. The sole importance of the bread suffering uncleanliness is that it defiles anyone who eats it.

> Mishnah Kelim 8.10. If a man touched one that had contracted uncleanness from a corpse, and he had foodstuffs or liquids in his mouth, and he put his head into the air-space of an oven that was clean, they render the oven unclean. If a man was clean and had foodstuffs or liquids in his mouth, and he put his head into the air-space of an oven that was unclean, they become unclean. If a man ate fig-cakes with unwashed hands and put his hand into his mouth to take out the small stones, R. Meir declares [the fig-cake] unclean, and R. Judah declares it clean. R. Jose says: If he turned it over in his mouth it becomes unclean; otherwise it remains clean. If he had a *pondion* in his mouth, R. Jose says: If it was to relieve his thirst, it becomes unclean.[10]

The oven that is rendered unclean here suffers only "derived uncleanness,"[11] that is, it does not convey uncleanness to other vessels directly but does to a liquid. But that liquid in its turn can convey uncleanliness to other vessels,[12] which in their turn can convey uncleanness.

> Mishnah Kelim 8.3. If a creeping thing was found beneath the bottom of an oven, the oven remains clean, since I may suppose that it was still alive when it fell, and is only now dead.

The point is that if the creeping thing was alive when it fell, it was not contaminating when it was in the oven's air-space.

> Mishnah Tohoroth 2.6. Second-grade uncleanness in common food renders unclean liquid that is common food, and renders invalid foods that are Heave offering.

Liquids are more susceptible to contracting uncleanness than is solid food. In this case the liquid becomes unclean with first-grade uncleanness.[13]

> Mishnah Tohoroth 10.7. If a man emptied out the cistern and in the first jarfull was found a creeping thing, all that is in the cistern is accounted unclean; if it was found in the last, that is unclean but the other are accounted clean. This applies only when he drew out the wine into each single jar; but if he emptied it out with a ladling-jar, and the creeping thing was found in one of the jars, it alone is accounted unclean. This applies only if he examined [the vessels] but did not cover up [the jars and the cistern], or if he covered them up but did not examine them. If he both examined them and covered them up, and the creeping thing was found in one jar, all is accounted unclean; all that is in the cistern is unclean, and all that is in the ladling-jar is unclean.

I do not think further examples are needed to show that, in the time of the Mishnah, rabbinical exegesis involved the idea that foods and liquids not proscribed expressly by God as part of a prohibited species could easily be unclean and thus defile the consumer.

The Mishnah was composed around A.D. 200, and it represents the discussions and debates of the rabbis who were the successors of the Pharisees of Jesus' time.[14] The evidence is thus considerably later than the lifetime of Jesus. It might then be suggested, as it has been in other contexts such as the composition of the Sanhedrin, that the Mishnah does not provide good evidence for the early first century.[15] Any such suggestion would be unconvincing. I should emphasize that my point here is not whether the examples from the Mishnah that I have quoted give the law exactly as it was understood in the time of Jesus but only that they indicate that the Pharisees held that food otherwise pure could become unclean and so defile the consumer. The issue of uncleanness is one that continues to this day. Such a tradition does not grow up in a short time, and we have abundant evidence from the Gospels themselves that the Pharisees were deeply involved in legal religious subtleties.

Of course, the Pharisees did not invent from nothing the idea that food otherwise clean could become unclean by contamination; they had scriptural authority. The most important source is perhaps Leviticus 2.19: "Flesh that touches any unclean thing shall not be eaten: it shall be burned up. As for other flesh, all who are clean may eat such flesh." But the prohibition in context is very narrow. The flesh in question is that of a thanksgiving sacrifice to God.[16] Still, it is obvious from experience that a concern for ritual cleanliness may lead to elaboration far beyond the original commands of prohibition.[17] Persons outside the tradition may well react with bewilderment and even antagonism.

Still, it is possibly a more daunting task to show that it is plausible that Jesus was denying defilement caused by consumption of such food. The first step is to show how weak the textual evidence is that Jesus declared food clean that was declared unclean by God.

The episode in Mark is otherwise recorded only by Matthew 15.10ff.

> Then he called the crowd to him and said to them, "Listen and understand: 11. it is not what goes into the mouth that defiles a person, but it is what comes out of the mouth that defiles." 12. Then the disciples approached and said to him, "Do you know that the Pharisees took offense when they heard what you said?" 13. He answered, "Every plant that my heavenly Father has not planted will be uprooted. 14. Let them alone; they are blind guides of the blind. And if one blind person guides another, both will fall into a pit." 15. But Peter said to him, "Explain this parable to us." 16. Then he said, "Are you also still without understanding? 17. Do you not see that whatever goes into the mouth enters the stomach, and goes out into the sewer? 18. But what comes out of the mouth proceeds from the heart, and this is what defiles. 19. For out of the heart come evil intentions, murder, adultery, fornication, theft, false witness, slander. 20. These are what defile a person, but to eat with unwashed hands does not defile.

Nothing is said here about Jesus declaring *all* food to be clean. What we are told in verse 12 is that the Pharisees had taken offense. But if Jesus meant that God's commandment was to be ignored, then all, not just Pharisees, would have been offended.

Even more to the point, Mark 7.19 does not in fact say, "Thus he declared all foods clean." The Greek καθαρίζων πάντα τὰ βρώματα contains nothing akin to "he declared." The problem emerges clearly when we look at the discussion by C. S. Mann. He translates, "So (by saying this) he declared all things clean." [18] But he candidly admits to a difficulty: "But the translation we have given depends upon supplying 'by saying this.'" [19] But any such interpretation is impossible in the absence of something like "he declared" or "by saying this"—and there is no justification for their addition. The Greek that I have quoted is better translated literally, "purging all meats," as in the King James Version: "Because it [food] entereth not into his heart, but into the belly, and goeth out into the draught, purging all meats." The text is dealing with the physical effects: what is eaten is purged by the body. Still, whether one takes as the correct reading *καθαρίζον* or *καθαρίζων* "purging," the phrase cannot properly be construed. Not surprisingly, editors usually take the phrase not as relating words used by Jesus but as an interpolation of the evangelist [20] or an early gloss. [21]

What matters to us is that the text does not claim that Jesus declared all food to be clean—only that what is eaten does not defile. That is a much weaker proposition. It does not define what is eaten. Jesus' meaning is to be dependent on context. And I would maintain, as already suggested, that in the absence of any sign of outrage, Jesus was not understood to be contradicting God's commandment that some types of food were unclean by their very nature. Matthew 15.20 is revealing: the food that does not defile is not declared to be pork or lobster but that eaten with unwashed hands. This seems akin to Mishnah Kelim 8.10 and putting unwashed hands into one's mouth while eating fig-cakes.

A second approach to the problem is that, as already noted, this declaration of Jesus is not used in the debate over whether Gentile Christians are obliged to obey Jewish food laws. Particularly significant is Colossians 2.16f.

Therefore do not let anyone condemn you in matters of food and drink or of observing festivals, new moons, or sabbaths.

17. These are only a shadow of what is to come, but the substance belongs to Christ.

Paul's letter is to bolster the faith of the addressees, which was being undermined by opponents whose false teaching demanded among other things observance of food regulations, festivals, new moons, and the Sabbath. These opponents were apparently Christians, not Jews or unbelieving Gentiles.[22] Thus, it is important to note that Jesus' pronouncement is not cited in support.

My argument is simple. Jesus showed ever-increasing hostility to the Pharisaic interpretation of God's law. Still, a declaration by Jesus that all food was clean is too opposed to God's detailed emphatic prohibition of certain foods to be plausible. Nor indeed is such a declaration clearly set out in either Matthew or Mark. But Jesus must have said something (or been thought to have said something) about food that was regarded as unclean being clean. In context Jesus' words should be seen as opposing certain interpretations of God's ban. Once again, he was showing hostility to the stance of the Pharisees. The issue became wider when the question arose as to whether the Levitical ban applied to Gentiles who became Christian (Acts 10.9ff.). Indeed, Paul took Jesus to mean that God was declaring Gentiles to be neither profane nor unclean (Acts 10.25ff., 11.1ff.). From an early date Jesus was understood as declaring all food clean. I would link this with the belief that his message was also to the Gentiles.

I have insisted that my overall approach to understanding the Gospels is textual and that I eschew rejecting the texts in favor of "what must have been." My approach here is no different. To interpret a text involves placing it in its original context. For me the context of Jesus' declaration was the belief of the Pharisees that food not declared unclean by God could become unclean by contamination. A contemporary example may be useful. If I, a resident of Washville, say in Washville, "Never take an H bus: the route is dangerous," my claim is absolute. But no one would understand me as claiming one should never take an H bus in Athens, Sparta, or Rome, Georgia. It would not occur to Jesus that he would be believed to have declared clean food that had expressly been declared unclean by God.

7

✛

THE
TRIAL
OF
JESUS

✛ ✛ ✛

IT IS MY BELIEF, STATED OR IMPLIED MORE THAN ONCE, THAT one cannot pick and choose bits here and there from among the Gospels. One account must be established as giving the most plausible tradition, then the others can be used as makeweights. I have insisted from the beginning of this book that I believe Mark gives us the most satisfactory early tradition for Jesus. Nowhere is this as clear as in the discussions of the trials of Jesus. Hence I will begin with Mark, go on to John and the other Synoptics, and then show the superior plausibility of Mark. In the interest of simplicity I will leave aside until the end two important and contested issues: that the crime Jesus was charged with before the Sanhedrin was blasphemy, and that the Sanhedrin had the power to put him to death.

In Mark 14 Jesus and his disciples after their Passover dinner went to a place called Gethsemane (14.32). Judas, one of the twelve disciples, arrived with an armed crowd from the chief priests, the scribes, and the elders, and they arrested Jesus (14.43). This was not a rabble.[1] Nor is there any sign that Roman soldiers were involved. One of those persons who were standing by drew his sword and cut off the ear of the high priest's slave (14.47). That individual is not specifically identified as one of the disciples. Jesus complained that they had come with swords and clubs to arrest him as if he were a bandit, and that he had been with them, teaching in the Temple, and they had not arrested him then (14.48f). Jesus' disciples deserted him and fled (14.50). The crowd seems to have made little or no determined attempt to arrest the disciples, although one young man who was following him was seized, but he escaped leaving his one piece of clothing behind (14.50ff).[2] We may confidently assume that the arrest was made at night because the leaders feared that Jesus' recent popularity with the crowd continued and that there might be trouble. This is spelled out at Mark 14.1f.:

> The chief priests and the scribes were looking for a way to arrest Jesus by stealth and kill him: 2. for they said, "Not during the festival or there may be a riot among the people."

Jesus was taken to the high priest, and all the chief priests, elders, and scribes were assembled (14.53).[3] We are told that the chief priests and the whole council were looking for testimony to put Jesus to death (14.55). This points to a formal meeting of the Sanhedrin, the highest assembly or court of the Jews. Indeed, the word used in Mark 14.55 for council is $\sigma\upsilon\nu\acute{\epsilon}\delta\rho\iota o\nu$. As we shall see later, any such meeting would have been illegal. The Sanhedrin probably could not meet in a private house (Mishnah Sanhedrin 11.2.); certainly, it could not meet at night in a capital case (Mishnah Sanhedrin 4.1). Many gave false testimony against Jesus, and their statements did not agree (Mark 14.56). The only false accusation against him that is spelled out is that Jesus said he would destroy the Temple and within three days would build another that was not made by hands (14.57f). Even here their testimony did not agree (14.58). Requirements of proof before the Sanhedrin were very strict: Two eyewitnesses who agreed on every point were required (Mishnah Sanhedrin 5.1ff.). The clear meaning of what Mark says is that the court did not have the evidence to convict Jesus. But, it must be asked, if the judges were going to insist on keeping to the strict requirements of proof, why did the Sanhedrin act so precipitously and illegally by holding the trial at night? The answer is that the chief priests and Pharisees had been desperate to arrest Jesus and get the whole business over with since the cleansing of the Temple but were afraid to act during Passover because of the crowd. Still, their integrity had not entirely disappeared.

The high priest intervened and asked Jesus for his response (Mark 14.60). Jesus made none (14.61).[4] The high priest asked if Jesus were the Messiah, and he replied that he was (14.61f). The high priest then tore his clothes and asked why witnesses would still be needed when they had heard his blasphemy, and he asked for their decision. All condemned him as deserving death (14.63–65). These three verses are particularly significant. They indicate that up to this point the evidence against Jesus was insufficient. But the high priest took the initiative and continued with the claim that Jesus' admission that he was the Messiah was blasphemous. That statement of Jesus probably was technically blasphemy at that time.[5] The high priest continued his initiative and tore his clothes. The point here is that the members of the council were obliged to rend their garments when someone was being found guilty of blasphemy. This is a sign of mourning. It is sometimes suggested that the high priest's action is not significant with regard to a verdict because Jews tore their clothes at other times of mourning. This interpretation is impossible. In a trial in which the high priest declared the accused to be blasphemous, the only possible symbolism of his tearing his clothes is condemnation of the accused. But then, it has been argued, all the judges should have torn their garments, not only the high priest. And he has done so at the wrong time, before condemnation to death at the second, morning session, which is the point of time specified in Mishnah Sanhedrin 7.5. Just so. The drama of Mark's account has been missed. The scenario is this. Although the meeting of the Sanhedrin was illegal, the judges insisted on observing the proper standards of evidence. On this basis, they could not reach a conviction. The high priest took matters into his own hands. He claimed that Jesus' admission in front of the council that he was the Messiah was blasphemy, asked what was the point of hearing other witnesses, and tore his clothes. He was acting as if Jesus were already condemned to death! And the Sanhedrin acquiesced in his conduct and decided Jesus was worthy of death. High-handed bullying by the boss paid off, as it so often does. The underlings had the choice: face up to the hard-nosed chief and cause a confrontation, or else submit. That in itself is always a difficult choice, and in this case the chief priests had no reason to be enthusiastic about Jesus anyway.

But there is much more to the issue of the high priest's high-handedness. The high priest was forbidden to rend his garments, and that not as a result of interpretation of Scripture but by Scripture itself. Leviticus 21.10 reads:

> The priest who is exalted above his fellows, on whose head the anointing oil has been poured and who has been consecrated to wear the vestments, shall not dishevel his hair, nor tear his vestments.[6]

The high priest's behavior is outrageous. He engages in a show of grief that is forbidden him but is obligatory on his fellows. On this basis, only the most bitter and obdurate of the judges would refuse to follow him.

When it was morning, the chief priests consulted with the elders and scribes and the whole council (Mark 15.1). This is presumably in terms of the very important rule of Mishnah Sanhedrin 5.5: "If they found him innocent, they set him free; otherwise they leave his sentence over until the morrow." The same rule stated that they should come together early in the morning. Mark does not tell us what sentence was decided upon, or even whether they decided upon a sentence at all. But they delivered Jesus, bound, to Pontius Pilate.

At this point I should like to pause again to show that there is no indication in Mark that Jesus was in any way an enemy of the Romans. Indeed, the evidence is all to the contrary.[7] In Mark Roman soldiers were not involved in Jesus' arrest. No real attempt was made by the arresters to catch the disciples, which they would have done if the arresters had been soldiers and the disciples were the band of a revolutionary leader. Jesus' main hostility was directed against the Pharisees rather than the Sadducees, yet the latter were more openly collaborators with the Romans. In fact, the Pharisees were intent on preserving a particular Jewish way of life and separateness: this was at least part of the reason that the crowds admired them. Then, when asked directly, Jesus did not reply that it was illegal to pay tax to the Romans (Mark 12.13ff.). Yet the supposed illegality of paying that tax appears to be the first ground of the Zealots' hatred of the Romans.[8] Significantly, too, Jesus had a disciple called something like Simon the Zealot (3.18). This would be impossible if they were all Zealots. One would not call a Scot living in Scotland "David the Scot," but if David emigrated to the United States he might be thought of in his place of residence there as "David the Scot." Such appellations indicate a characteristic that separates the individual from his fellows.[9]

One should, of course, go further. There is no sign in any of the Gospels that Jesus was a revolutionary against the Romans. To me it is inconceivable if he had been that all trace could have been successfully excised.[10] There is an even greater proof. Jesus appears in the Roman historians, Tacitus and Suetonius, and in the Jewish Josephus, who had gone over to the Romans. Tacitus records:

> Therefore, to suppress this rumor [that he was responsible for the burning of Rome], Nero supplied scapegoats and tortured with the most exquisite punishments those whom the vulgar called Christians and who were hated for their depravity. The founder of this group, Christ, had been executed in the reign of Tiberius by the procurator, Pontius Pilate. The deadly superstition was repressed for the time being, but broke out afresh, not only through Judaea, the birth-place of this evil but even in the city [Rome] where all disgusting and shameful practices collect and flourish on all sides. (*Annales* 15.44)

Josephus has this:

> *Jewish Antiquities* 18.63. About this time there lived Jesus, a wise man, if indeed one ought to call him a man, for he was a doer of marvelous feats, a teacher of such people as receive the truth with pleasure. He drew over to him many Jews and many Greeks. He was the Messiah. 64. When Pilate, upon hearing him accused by men of the highest standing among us, had condemned him to be crucified, those that loved him at the first did not give up this affection for him. For on the third day he appeared to them alive again, for the divine prophets had prophesied these and ten thousand other wonderful things about him. And the tribe of the Christians, so-called after him, has still not disappeared to this day.[11]

Not a word of hostility on the part of Jesus to the Romans.[12]

To return to the narrative, Jesus was delivered to Pilate. According to Mark, Pilate took the initiative and asked Jesus if he were king of the Jews (Mark 15.2). So Pilate must have had some prior knowledge of what was afoot. Of course he had. The procurator's consent was in practice needed before the Sanhedrin could meet.[13] Jesus replied, "You say so." Basically this is the same as refusing to answer. The chief priests then accused him of many things (15.3). Mark does not state, however, that they told Pilate that they had tried him, or had found him guilty, or had condemned him to death. Pilate then wanted Jesus to respond to what he termed the "many charges they bring against you" (15.4). The words indicate that for Mark the chief priests had not claimed to have convicted Jesus but had simply brought to Pilate accusations against him. Jesus made no answer to Pilate (15.5). The next few verses show that the immediate procedure had ended and that Pilate had made his decision.[14] Jesus, as we shall shortly see, is clearly treated as a prisoner who might be mercifully released, but in fact he is crucified for sedition, treason against the Roman emperor.

But can it be claimed that there has been a proper Roman trial of a non-Roman before a provincial governor? The answer is a resounding yes, and for that we have the clearest possible evidence, though from a slightly later period.[15] Pliny the Younger was governor of Bythinia from around A.D. 100 to 102, and he wrote from there to the emperor Trajan for advice about the trials of persons who were supposed to be Christians:

> In the meantime, I have followed this approach with regard to those who were denounced to me as Christians. I asked them whether they were Christians. I asked those who confessed a second time and a third time, having threatened torture. Those who still persevered I ordered to be executed. For I did not doubt, whatever their faith was, that their pertinacity and inflexible obstinacy deserved punishment. (*Epistulae* 10.96)

The offense under consideration by Pliny was to be a Christian; that charged against Jesus was the more serious crime of treason.

Earlier in the letter Pliny had expressed uncertainty as to whether being a Christian was by itself the crime.[16] Now he is saying in effect that whether or not it was a crime, if an accused person admitted three times that he was so objectionable, he deserved to be, and would be, executed. To refuse to reply to Pilate's question was to show equal obstinacy. And Pliny, in contrast to Pilate, has the reputation for moderation and fair-mindedness.[17] Moreover, Jesus was not a Roman citizen, so Pilate had no need to respect the niceties reserved for them in a capital trial. From the Roman point of view, Jesus was a *peregrinus,* a foreigner.[18]

What is going on at this stage in Mark is clear. When the Sanhedrin met in the morning to give their official verdict, enough of the judges were ashamed of the illegality of the trial, of the failure of appropriate evidence, of their acceptance of the high priest's outrageous bullying, and of the verdict of blasphemy, or they were afraid of the mob, that they refused to convict. No other scenario would explain why they did not put Jesus to death by stoning but instead handed him over to Pilate for whom blasphemy was no crime.[19] The charge used against Jesus by Pilate was treason to the Roman emperor, and he was properly tried and put to death. But in the final analysis he was not convicted of any capital offense by the Sanhedrin, and he was not executed by the Jews. In Mark, the failure of the Sanhedrin to convict is played down. (Indeed, the evangelist may not have been conscious of it.)

The account in John is very different. Jesus returned to Judaea (11.7) and raised Lazarus from the dead (11.11ff). Some who saw him told Pharisees (11.46), and they and the chief priests called a meeting of the Sanhedrin (11.47). There it was claimed that if the people believed in Jesus, the Romans would destroy both the holy place and the nation (11.48). The high priest, Caiaphas, who was a Sadducee (or he would not have been the high priest), declared it was expedient that one man die for the nation (11.50).

Jesus went to Ephraim (11.54) but returned to Bethany six days before the Passover (12.1). The chief priests planned to put the risen Lazarus to death, too (12.10).

After the Last Supper Jesus went across the Kidron Valley with his disciples (18.1). Judas brought a detachment of soldiers together with police from the chief priests and Pharisees, and they arrested Jesus (18.3ff.). The soldiers were led by an officer with the rank of military tribune. This is the first mention in the Gospels of Roman involvement. They took Jesus not to the Roman praetorium but to the house of Annas, who was Caiaphas's father-in-law (18.13) and a respected former high priest. This can be plausibly explained. Presumably despite the arrest involving Roman troops, Pilate was reluctant to be involved in a matter that could lead to rioting, and in any event the chief priests wanted to examine Jesus. That the Romans were less than enthusiastic in the arrest is clear from the fact that they made no attempt to arrest the disciples. Annas sent Jesus, bound, to Caiaphas (18.24). Early in the morning they took Jesus to Pilate's headquarters (18.28). Nothing in the account indicates that Jesus was formally tried by the Sanhedrin, and the earlier meeting of which we are told, before the arrest, was a council session, not a trial. The Sanhedrin could not lawfully hold a capital trial at night or, probably, in a private house. Accordingly, for John we have no need to enquire into the crime Jesus was charged with before the Sanhedrin.[20]

Pilate asked those who brought Jesus what crime he was charged with (18.29). They gave no straight answer but only said that if Jesus were not a criminal they would not have delivered him to Pilate (18.30) and that they were not permitted to put anyone to death (18.32). This last statement, I believe, is incorrect. Pilate asked Jesus whether he was a king and received no answer. This obduracy, no matter what the charge, would be enough to explain the sentence of flogging and crucifixion. An almost exact parallel, as we have seen, is in Pliny *Epistolae* 10.96. Still, in light of the questions put and of the inscription on the cross, Jesus was put to death for high treason (*maiestas*).

Matthew is again different. After the Passover dinner Jesus went with his disciples to Gethsemane (26.36). Judas arrived with a large crowd with swords and clubs, from the chief priests and the elders (26.47), and they arrested Jesus (26.50). One of the disciples drew his sword and cut off the ear of the high priest's servant (26.51). The disciples deserted and fled (26.56). No mention is made of any attempt to arrest them. Those who arrested Jesus took him to the house of Caiaphas, the high priest, where the scribes and elders were gathered (26.57). There was a meeting of the Sanhedrin (συνέδριον) (26.59), and we are expressly told they were looking for false testimony in order to put Jesus to death, but they found none, although many false witnesses came forward (26.60).[21] Then two witnesses claimed they had heard Jesus say he could destroy the Temple of God and rebuild it in three days. The high priest asked Jesus for his response, but he gave none (26.63). The high priest asked if he were the Messiah,[22] took his answer—"You have said it"—as positive, then tore his clothes and said, "He has blasphemed! Why do we still need witnesses? You have now heard his blasphemy. What is your verdict?" (26.65f.). They answered, "He deserves death" (26.66). So Jesus was tried by the Sanhedrin and convicted.

In the morning, they all met again and conferred how to bring about Jesus' death. Then they bound him and handed him over to Pilate (Matthew 27.1f). Nothing is said about whether they again found him guilty and fixed his sentence. Only at this stage in Matthew do Romans become involved.

But Matthew now inserts an episode that was not in Mark and that is illuminating for Matthew's understanding, although not part of the events leading up to Jesus' arrest, the arrest itself, the trial and execution:

27.3. When Judas, his betrayer, saw that Jesus was condemned, he repented and brought back the thirty pieces of silver to the chief priests and the elders. 4. He said, "I have sinned by betraying innocent blood." But they said, "What is that to us? See to it yourself." 5. Throwing down the pieces of silver in the temple, he departed; and he went and hanged himself. 6. But the chief priests, taking the pieces of silver, said, "It is not lawful to put them into the treasury, since they are blood money." 7. After conferring together, they used them to buy the potter's field as a place to bury foreigners. 8. For this reason that field has been called the Field of Blood to this day. 9. Then was fulfilled what had been spoken through the prophet Jeremiah. "And they took the thirty pieces of silver, the price of the one on whom a price had been set, on whom some of the people of Israel had set a price, 10. and they gave them for the potter's field, as the Lord commanded me."

Full of remorse, Judas admitted to the chief priests and elders that he had betrayed an innocent man. When the authorities refused to have anything to do with the matter, he hanged himself. The point of this is that under rabbinic law a bearer of false evidence should suffer the penalty appropriate to the supposed crime: in this case, death.[23] Judas is acting as if Jesus had been condemned. Indeed, Matthew 27.3 says, "Judas seeing . . . that he was condemned" (ἰδὼν ᾽Ιούδας. . .ὅτι κατεκρίθη). So for Matthew the Sanhedrin had confirmed its verdict, although this emerges only in a very indirect way.[24]

But Jesus was now before Pilate, who asked if he were the king of the Jews, and Jesus replied, "You say so" (Matthew 27.11). The chief priests and elders now accused him, and he answered nothing (27.12). Pilate asked if he had heard the many accusations, and again he did not respond (27.13f.). This amounts to a trial before the Roman governor, with the priests and elders bringing accusations against Jesus, not a religious trial verdict and sentence. Any trial before Pilate would be on secular issues. There is thus confusion in Matthew: conviction of Jesus by the Sanhedrin but no execution, followed by conviction by Pilate and execution.

In Luke 22, shortly before the Passover the chief priests and scribes were looking for a way to kill Jesus, yet they were afraid of the people (22.1f). Judas discussed with the chief priests and officers of the Temple police how to betray Jesus, and they paid him (22.3ff). After Passover dinner Jesus went with his disciples to the Mount of Olives (22.39). Judas came leading a crowd (22.47). Those around Jesus asked if they should draw their swords, and one cut off the ear of the high priest's slave (22.49ff.). With the crowd were the chief priests, the officers of the Temple police, and the elders of the people who had come for Jesus (22.52).

They seized him and took him to the house of the high priest (22.56). There is no indication in Luke that there was a meeting of the Sanhedrin that night, although Jesus was mocked and beaten (22.65).[25]

> 22.66. When day came, the assembly of the elders of the people, both chief priests and scribes, gathered together, and they brought him to their council. 67. They said, "If you are the Messiah, tell us." He replied, "If I tell you, you will not believe; 68. and if I question you, you will not answer. 69. But from now on the Son of Man will be seated at the right hand of the power of God." 70. All of them asked, "Are you, then, the Son of God?" He said to them, "You say that I am." 71. Then they said, "What further testimony do we need? We have heard it ourselves from his own lips!"

Thus, in the morning there was a trial session before the Sanhedrin. They decided he was guilty, but we are not told that they passed sentence. If they had, that behavior would have been contrary to law, since sentencing had to wait until the day after the trial, and there had been no trial during the night.

They took Jesus to Pilate and accused him: he was perverting their nation, forbidding them to pay taxes to the emperor, and claiming that he was the Messiah, a king (23.1f.). Pilate asked Jesus if he were the king of the Jews (23.3). There is, thus, a divergence here from Mark and Matthew, in which Pilate seemed to know that Jesus was said to be the king of the Jews before accusations were made.

Jesus replied, "You say so," and Pilate found no charge against him. Pilate, as in Mark and Matthew, was reluctant to condemn Jesus, but this time he tried to pass the buck by sending Jesus to Herod Antipas, who was then in Jerusalem (23.6ff.).[26] Herod sent him back. Pilate still tried to release Jesus, but eventually crucified him. The inscription on the cross read: "This is the king of the Jews" (23.38). So the crime for which he was put to death was treason.[27]

But why, it must be asked, did Jesus not defend himself before Pilate? To Pilate's question, "Are you the king of the Jews?" Jesus replied, "You say so" (Mark 15.2; Matthew 27.11). This was the best that Jesus could do because he was unwilling to deny his status. Commentators take Jesus' "You say so" as a strong yes,[28] but, as David Daube has shown, it is deliberately ambiguous.[29]

The central issue for us is the nature of the trial proceedings, if any, before the Sanhedrin, and here in the three Synoptics we have three very different versions, all of which show the Sanhedrin acting in an illegal way. The one indisputable fact about Jesus' life is that he was executed by the Romans in a Roman manner, crucifixion, for a secular Roman crime, sedition or treason. But if the Sanhedrin had condemned Jesus to death for a religious crime, it would be for Jews to carry out the sentence. Yet in Matthew the

Sanhedrin condemns Jesus, so the Romans should not carry out the execution in a non-Jewish way. There is no reason for the Sanhedrin not to carry out the sentence. And Pilate, it must be stressed, is most reluctant to be involved. In Luke, the members of the Sanhedrin find Jesus guilty of blasphemy on the morning after his arrest. But having gone to that trouble, they do not wait to reconvene the following day to confirm the verdict and to pass sentence. Instead, they hand him over to Pilate, saying that he was perverting their nation, forbidding them to pay taxes, and claiming to be a king. Again it must be stressed that Pilate was most reluctant to get involved. The scenario in Luke is possible but very implausible. In Mark, the Sanhedrin convicts Jesus in the illegal trial at night but apparently reverses itself in the morning. So it could not execute Jesus. It hands Jesus over to Pilate with accusations, and Pilate tries him and, still with much hesitation, executes him for a secular crime. Only the version in Mark can both account for the course of events and be plausible. Hence I conclude that it is more likely to be close to the truth than the versions in Matthew and Luke. I therefore discount Matthew and Luke as evidence of the main course of events leading up to the execution of Jesus. Still, that does not mean that, in points of detail, one or the other may not be more accurate than Mark. Nor am I suggesting that the tradition that did not fully accept Mark's version was in any way being deliberately misleading.

I wish to point out the contrast between the three Synoptics over Jesus' trials. In Mark the Sanhedrin tried Jesus for blasphemy (14.53ff.), the witnesses were insufficient in their testimony (14.56ff.), the high priest intervened, saying they had heard blasphemy (14.63), and the judges found him guilty (14.64). At the necessary meeting the following morning they did not confirm their sentence, but they took Jesus to Pilate, who asked him if he were the king of the Jews (15.1ff.). So Pilate was investigating a secular crime against the Romans. In Matthew, in contrast, the witnesses were sufficient (26.60), although the high priest also intervened violently (26.63ff.) but illogically. From the episode with Judas (27.3ff.) we know that at the morning session (27.1), Matthew accepted that the judges had condemned Jesus. The evidence, though, is so indirect that we may suspect it was the evangelist's opinion that the Sanhedrin had convicted but that this was not clear in his sources on the trial. The judges delivered him to Pilate, who questioned Jesus on the same secular issue as in Mark. In Luke there was only a morning session (22.66ff.). There is no emphasis on lack of witnesses: the stress is all on whether Jesus claimed to be the Messiah. The Sanhedrin took Jesus before Pilate and accused him: "We found this man perverting our nation, forbidding us to pay taxes to the emperor, and saying that he himself is the Messiah, a king" (23.2). Of these three accusations before the Roman procurator, the first pertains to the religious offense of leading a town astray and this, according to Mishnah Sanhedrin 7.4, is punishable by death by stoning. Perverting the Jewish nation is no crime against Roman law.[30] The third accusation as it is recorded is also primarily of a religious offense. But Pilate's interest is in the Roman crime of sedition, and he asks Jesus if he is the king of the Jews (23.2).

In this context only Mark tells the story plausibly. Thus, in Matthew, there was no need (as there was in Mark) for the high priest to rend his garment inappropriately and illegally: he already had the necessary witnesses. In Luke it was pointless to have the Sanhedrin accuse Jesus of a purely religious offense in front of Pilate. Insofar as Matthew and Luke here depend on Mark, they have again weakened the dynamics of the course of events, due to a lack of understanding. We can be confident this time that we do not have an instance where Mark has deliberately heightened the drama, whereas Matthew or Luke is closer to the original tradition. It is in Matthew that the high priest's tearing of his clothes is quite pointless although dramatic; in Mark it has a fundamental role. It is Luke that shows the Sanhedrin irrelevantly and uselessly charging Jesus with religious crimes before Pilate.

In all four Gospels Pilate was most reluctant to execute Jesus. Details are not needed here.[31] The reluctance is not to be seen as weakness or as a sense of justice, qualities not typical of Pilate.[32] Rather, like the Jewish leaders, he was afraid of a riot led by supporters of Jesus. After all, a prime part of his office was to have the peace kept. But once he had convinced himself that the crowd favored Jesus' death, he had no hesitation. It is emphasized (by silence) that he was not much perturbed by Jesus' behavior.

We come at last to the crime with which Jesus was charged before the Sanhedrin and which I have declared to be blasphemy.[33] At Mark 14.64, after Jesus admitted he was the Messiah, the high priest said, "You have heard the blasphemy" (ἠκούσατε τῆς βλασφημίας). Matthew 26.65 has "He blasphemed (ἐβλασφή-μσεν). No other charge is mentioned. The words used can refer to no crime other than blasphemy. But some scholars see a problem. First, the Greek words that give rise to our *blasphemy* and *to blaspheme* have a wider meaning and include defamation or insult.[34] Second and more important, Mishnah Sanhedrin 7.5 relates that blasphemy is committed solely by uttering the name of God. The point at issue is the accuracy of the Mishnah for the time of Jesus. We should hold that in this, as in some other regards, the Mishnah, as is generally agreed,[35] did not set forth the legal system of the Sanhedrin as it was before A.D. 70, but represents an ideal, with the awesome crime being reduced in scope. Certainly, the Sanhedrin was not at that time a council of scholars as it is represented in the Mishnah but was composed of an amalgam of hereditary members and scholars, as it appears in the Gospels and Josephus.[36] I should not be understood as suggesting that the Mishnah is generally an unreliable source for law in the time of Jesus. This individual misrepresentation of the Sanhedrin in the Mishnah, it should be noted, is particularly understandable. After the destruction of the Temple, the Sadducees were no longer a powerful force. The tradition in the Mishnah is specifically that of the Pharisees, who were the scholars. It would be tempting to represent the Sanhedrin as always having been a council of scholars.

The penalty for blasphemy was death by stoning (Mishnah Sanhedrin 7.4).[37] But the issue is controversial because of John 18.31: "Pilate said to them, 'Take him yourself, and judge him according to your law.' The Jews replied, 'We are not permitted to put anyone to death.'" The second part of the text is unambiguous, but it cannot be correct. On other occasions, too, John shows ignorance of important Jewish customs.[38] John 18.31 is the only plausible evidence that the Jews were not permitted to put anyone to death, but it is immediately contradicted by John 19.6 where Pilate is made to say, "Take him yourselves and crucify him: I find no case against him." Not only that, but in the first part of John 18.31, Pilate is represented as being unaware that the Sanhedrin could not condemn to death. Moreover, not only does Sanhedrin 7.5 list the crimes (including blasphemy) for which death by stoning was the appropriate penalty but Mishnah Sanhedrin 6.1ff. sets out in great detail the mode of execution. It is inconceivable to me that scholars would simply make up such detailed imaginary rules. Then both Philo[39] and Josephus[40] show that the Sanhedrin could execute people, even non-Jews, even Roman citizens, for entering the sanctuary of the Temple. If the Sanhedrin could put non-Jews to death for one offense, it is difficult to accept it had not capital jurisdiction over Jews in other religious matters. Josephus relates that the Sanhedrin executed Jesus' brother James and some others by stoning.[41] Paul indicates that he himself voted for the execution of early Christians.[42] He makes the claim twice: first before the

Jews (Acts 22.4) and then before King Agrippa (Acts 26.10). Even for as late as the third century, Origen writing to Africanus (letter 14) indicates that Jews under Roman rule were trying and executing Christians, although this was being done with little publicity.

(Still, I should like to modify my stance when I claimed in two earlier books that John's "We are not permitted to put anyone to death" was a gaffe.[43] I had not appreciated the full subtlety in John. The clue to a proper understanding lies in another text of Origen in the translation of Rufinus: "It cannot punish a murderer nor stone an adulteress, for the Roman power claims that for itself."[44] The position would be as I stated: "The Romans would have exclusive right to try secular capital cases; the Sanhedrin the exclusive right to try Jews for religious capital cases not involving a Roman criminal offense."[45]

To return to John. The Sanhedrin did not try Jesus. The leaders took Jesus to Pilate, who asked, "What accusation do you bring against the man?" (18.29). The leaders sidestep the issue and answer, "If this man were not a criminal, we would not have handed him over to you" (18.30). They do not state the crime of which they accuse Jesus. Pilate persists that they should try him themselves, and they reply that they are not permitted to put anyone to death.

They are pushing Pilate to try Jesus for a secular offense, the only kind that is of interest to Pilate. In that sense it would be true that they were not permitted to put anyone to death.)

8

✟

MIRACLES, TEACHING, AND PARABLES

✟ ✟ ✟

IT SHOULD BE NO SURPRISE THAT JESUS' MIRACLES, TEACHING, and parables as they appear in Mark can be treated together in a modern book like this in one chapter. In Mark Jesus' stock-in-trade is miracle working. In this Jesus shows a strong contrast with John the Baptist. Jesus' teaching is very much intertwined with his miracles. One might also say that in large measure his miracle working is at the center of his message. And whereas Mark often relates that Jesus taught, what he taught is usually not recorded. More than that, the meaning of his message is often obscure. He often taught in parables that were not easily comprehensible, and Jesus even observed that he intended not to be understood.[1]

The accuracy of much of the foregoing paragraph can be illuminated by a glance at a modern concordance such as Strong's.[2] A look under the heading "The Miracles of Jesus Christ" shows that Mark, the shortest of the Synoptics, contains as many miracles as the longer Matthew—for the most part the same ones—and almost as many as Luke. Those in Luke which are not in Mark are also missing from Matthew. John, as usual, has a different tradition: only two miracles are in both John and Mark. The others in John, relatively few in number, have no counterpart in the Synoptics. Under the heading "Teachings and Illustrations of Christ" appear few references in Strong's concordance to Mark, in contrast to Matthew and Luke.

Immediately after Jesus' baptism and his retreat to and return from the desert he collected disciples.

> 1.21. They went to Capernaum; and when the sabbath came, he entered the synagogue and taught. 22. They were astounded at his teaching, for he taught them as one having authority, and not as the scribes. 23. Just then there was in their synagogue a man with an unclean spirit, 24. and he cried out, "What have you to do with us, Jesus of Nazareth? Have you come to destroy us? I know who you are, the Holy One of God." 25. But Jesus rebuked him, saying, "Be silent, and come out of him!" 26. And the unclean spirit, convulsing him and crying with a loud voice, came out of him. 27. They were all amazed, and they kept on asking one another, "What is this? A new teaching—with authority! He commands even the unclean spirits, and they obey him."

Jesus' teaching came before his first miracle. People were astonished at his teaching, "for he taught them as one having authority, and not as the scribes." A distinction is being drawn: Jesus taught like a rabbi, as one ordained, not like the scribes.[3] Immediately thereafter, Jesus performed his first act of exorcism, by voice alone, driving out an unclean spirit. The people were amazed and asked one another, "What is this? A new teaching with authority? And he commands the unclean spirits and they obey him." The people were taking the exorcism as part of his teaching with authority. But the substantive content of his teaching is not revealed by Mark.

Mark's report of Jesus' teaching continues in this fashion. In Mark 1.38f. Jesus went through Galilee with his disciples, "proclaiming in their synagogues and expelling demons." Exorcism continues, as does his teaching, although we are not told what it is. Before this we had been told of two other miracles: Jesus cured Simon's mother-in-law, who had a fever (Mark 1.30f.), and many others who were sick or had demons (Mark 1.32ff.). The miracles are explicit, but the teaching is not. It appears that, for Mark, Jesus' miracle working is more important than any precise message he may have had.

Jesus cured the paralytic who had been let down to him through the roof (Mark 2.1ff.). The episode is recounted in detail: the crowd was so great that people could not get to see him; those bringing the paralyzed man therefore removed the roof and let down the man on his mat (Mark 2.4). This all happened when Jesus "was speaking the word to them" (Mark 2.2). But what the word was Mark does not reveal. Still, we are not left entirely in the dark. When Jesus saw the reaction of the scribes to his words "Son, your sins are forgiven" (Mark 2.5), he claimed that the Son of Man—by which he means himself—had authority to forgive sin. Thus, at this point, at the very least, Jesus was claiming to have the authority of God. But to show this authority he used a miracle.

At Mark 2.13 Jesus taught beside the sea, but we are not told what he taught. Again, in contrast, we have at Mark 1.40ff. a detailed account of his curing the leper but no sign of any specific teaching. When he cured the withered hand in the synagogue on the Sabbath (Mark 3.1ff.), he did have a spiritual message: that the Pharisaic observance of the Sabbath was harsh and overly rigid.

The emphasis continues to be on the miracles. From Mark

3.17ff. we learn that a great multitude was following him because of his cures. We are not told they followed him because of his message. I stress this because in Mark it happens only just before he enters Jerusalem near the Mount of Olives (Mark 11.8ff.) that he wins popular acclaim as something more than a miracle worker. I emphasize this because once again we are seeing a recognizable pattern in Mark: Jesus as miracle worker with unspecified teaching; Jesus then as miracle worker with an incomprehensible teaching; Jesus recognized late as the Messiah.

This pattern, it should be noticed, is much less prominent in Matthew and Luke. In Matthew 4 we find Jesus teaching, proclaiming the good news, and healing. "And they brought to him all who were ill, having various diseases and torments, possessed by demons, lunatics, paralyzed, and he healed them" (4.24). The teaching is again unspecified, but the miracles of healing, in contrast to Mark, are not detailed. But then, at the very beginning of the next chapter, Matthew 5, comes the beautiful, detailed—it occupies three whole chapters—teaching of the Sermon on the Mount. The first detailed miracle, the curing of the leper, which derives from Mark, occurs only at Matthew 8.1ff.

In Luke the teaching even comes first. At Luke 4.15 he began to teach in their synagogues and was praised by everyone. No mention of any miracles. Immediately thereafter, at verses 16ff. we have the first detailed information about his teaching. He read from the prophet Isaiah and declared that that teaching had been fulfilled in their hearing (4.21). When he told them that no prophet was accepted in his home town (4.23ff.), they were furious and wanted to throw him over the cliff (4.29). Clearly his teaching was unpersuasive. (But it is proper to acknowledge that there is more to the issue than a simple failure to accept Jesus' teaching. Jesus declared that no prophet was accepted in his home town.[4] Jesus had left as a respected citizen and now returned as an itinerant preacher with no obvious means of support. And, despite his reputation, he was unable to perform miracles.[5] No wonder his fellow townspeople were unimpressed.) Only subsequently do we have a miracle, and this derives from Mark (although it is not the same miracle with which Matthew begins). At Luke 4.31ff. he was teaching "with authority" in the synagogue, and then he cured the man with the unclean spirit. The episode is recounted much as in Mark.

We should not be surprised that Jesus could be regarded and esteemed as a miracle worker but as nothing more. Miracles and their makers were common in the ancient world and later.[6] In Mark itself (9.38ff.) we find someone who was not his follower casting out evil spirits in his name. In Acts 8.9ff. we are told of a man named Simon, not then a follower of Jesus, who practiced magic so successfully that he amazed the people of Samaria, and he declared that he was someone: "All of them, from the least to the greatest gave heed to him saying, 'This man is the power of God, which is called great'" (Acts 8.10). Jesus' first miracle in John (2.1ff.), turning water into wine, was one already well known to pagan religion and was associated with Dionysius, the discoverer of the vine.[7] Archeological evidence attests the miracle in Dionysiac religion in a temple at Corinth.[8] Vespasian under whom the Temple was destroyed in A.D. 70 was in Alexandria in 69 shortly after his troops had proclaimed him emperor. Two poor men, one lame, one blind, approached him as he sat on the tribunal, begging him to cure them. They said that the god Serapis had promised they would be cured if Vespasian spat in the blind man's eyes and if he touched the other's leg with his heel. Vespasian hesitated but was encouraged by friends, and before a large crowd he performed the miracles.[9] Thus, the emperor who destroyed the Jewish nation performed miracles similar to Jesus' greatest. Tacitus also records many miracles at that time in Alexandria that showed the gods' favor to Vespasian. More than that, a famous passage of Josephus describes Jesus as a doer of marvelous feats.[10] Yet the Christian Origen, who lived from around 185 to 255, expressly states twice that Josephus did not believe in Jesus as the Christ.[11]

Let us continue with Mark. Only at the beginning of Mark 4 do we have Jesus' first detailed teaching. Significantly it is a parable, that of the sower who went out to sow. The parable was incomprehensible, and Jesus knew it could not be understood. Indeed, astonishingly, Jesus meant it to be incomprehensible:

> 4.10. When he was alone, those who were around him along with the twelve asked him about the parables. 11. And he said to them, "To you has been given the secret of the kingdom of God, but for those outside, everything comes in parables; 12. in order that
>> 'they may indeed look, but not perceive,
>> and may indeed listen, but not understand;
>> so that they may not turn again and be forgiven.'"
> 13. And he said to them, "Do you not understand this parable? Then how will you understand all the parables?"

Even the disciples could not understand. The quotation is from Isaiah 6.9f., but the prophet's point is different, as I hope to show in chapter 12. Isaiah is menacing, but his point is redemption. Jesus emphatically does not have redemption in mind when he speaks, as he does, in parables:

> 4.33. With many such parables he spoke the word to them, as they were able to hear it; 34. he did not speak to them except in parables, but he explained everything in private to his disciples.

Only the elite inner circle was to be enlightened. Mark tells us he taught only in parables, and the very text indicates that this teaching was intended to be incomprehensible.

Even when Jesus taught in what was arguably not a parable, when he declared food clean that was considered unclean, he was incomprehensible (Mark 7.14ff.). When his disciples asked him about the parable, Jesus said, "So you, too, are without understanding" (Mark 7.18). The implication is, indeed, that Jesus knew that the crowd had not understood, and this can only have been his policy. In fact, the parable is incomprehensible. What is it that comes out of a man that defiles (Mark 7.16)? The obvious—but as he explains to the disciples, incorrect—meaning is excrement. But how could anyone understand that he was declaring food clean that was considered unclean? God's prohibition against eating unclean food was strong and explicit (Leviticus 11.10ff.). The moral issue underlying the parable, and which in any event had no need of a declaration that all food was clean, was explained only to the disciples.

We need not proceed further with Jesus' miracles, which continue until the end of his ministry. But a little more should be said about the nature of his teaching in Mark. He preached repentance (Mark 1.14), declared food clean that was considered unclean, argued against divorce, and otherwise taught, but only in the most general terms, the commandments of God: that fornication, theft, murder, adultery, avarice, wickedness, deceit, licentiousness, envy, slander, pride, and folly will corrupt. But specificity is not given (Mark 7.21f.). To the question of what was required to attain eternal life he replied:

> 10.19. "You know the commandments: 'You shall not murder; You shall not commit adultery; You shall not steal; You shall not bear false witness; You shall not defraud; Honor your father and mother.'" 20. He said to him, "Teacher, I have kept all these since my youth." 21. Jesus, looking at him, loved him and said, "You lack one thing; go, sell what

you own, and give the money to the poor, and you will have treasure in heaven; then come, follow me." 22. When he heard this, he was shocked and went away grieving, for he had many possessions.

Thus, in Mark Jesus taught the desirability and even the need for positive morality, but this is not stressed, as it is in Matthew and Luke. Mark's message is sharply focused: on the need for repentance, which is belief in Jesus as the Messiah, and the difficulty of being a true follower (Mark 10.29ff., 13.9ff.).[12]

9

✠

JESUS
AND THE
MESSIAH

✠ ✠ ✠

FOR MARK, JESUS RECOGNIZED HIMSELF AS THE MESSIAH AT his baptism or shortly thereafter. But this self-recognition does not seem to interest Jesus very much. In contrast, Jesus frequently proclaims himself with apparent pride to be the Son of Man.

Jesus first admits himself to be the Messiah at Mark 8.30. He had asked his disciples whom they said he was and Peter responded, "You are the Messiah" (Mark 8.29). Then we have the following verse: "And he sternly ordered them not to tell anyone about him." Thus, Jesus did not claim to be the Messiah but accepted the fact. More than that, he did not want it to be made known. Nonetheless, he had engineered some kind of answer from Peter to his question. Significantly Mark immediately continues: "Then he began to teach them that the Son of Man must undergo great suffering." Jesus is made to attach much more importance to his role as the Son of Man than to being the Messiah.

At Mark 12.35ff. Jesus puts the question, How can the scribes say the Messiah is the son of David? He then argues in a complex and unconvincing way from Psalm 110 that he will not be. As I claimed in chapter 1, the crowd's delight at this is because they believed Jesus had revealed himself as the Messiah. But it must be stressed again that Jesus had not claimed to be the Messiah. Nor, this time, had he admitted it. The crowd made the assumption from his argument.

The most instructive passage is Mark 13. Jesus forecast that the Temple would be destroyed, and his disciples asked when and what the sign would be that this would happen.

> 13.5. Then Jesus began to say to them, "Beware that no one leads you astray. 6. Many will come in my name and say, 'I am he!' and they will lead many astray."

He describes the desolation to come and continues:

> 13.21. "And if anyone says to you at that time, 'Look! Here is the Messiah!' or 'Look! There he is!'—do not believe it. 22. False messiahs and false prophets will appear and produce signs and omens, to lead astray, if possible, the elect."

Jesus explains that some will come claiming to be him, and he identifies them as false Messiahs. That is, Jesus is admitting that he is the Messiah but is not claiming it directly. But then he says the Son of Man, whom he has several times claimed to be, will come in great power and glory. The image of the Son of Man is emphasized whereas that of the Messiah is not.

Jesus also indirectly showed he believed he was the Messiah during the Last Supper (Mark 14.22ff.). At the end of the meal Jesus took a loaf of bread, broke it, gave it to the disciples and said, "Take, eat: this is my body."[1] As David Daube insists, if there had been no precedent for this, "his disciples—to put it mildly— would have been perplexed."[2] And Daube convincingly shows that the precedent was in the Passover liturgy.[3] In the liturgy, prior to the meal a portion of unleavened bread is broken off, taken from the table, and brought back at the end of the meal and distributed to the company as the last bit of food that night. Traditionally, this piece of bread is termed *Aphiqoman*. The word is not Semitic but the Greek αφικόμενος, or εφικόμενος, and it means "the coming one," or "he that cometh," and represents the Messiah. When Jesus at the conclusion of the meal breaks bread and says, "Take, eat: this is my body," he is saying to the disciples, "I am the Messiah." The Eucharist appears in Matthew, Mark, and Luke. But the importance of the Messiah for Jesus does not emerge, nor does he expressly declare he is the Messiah.

Jesus' last admission to being the Messiah is at his trial before the Sanhedrin:

> 14.61. Again the high priest asked him, "Are you the Messiah, the Son of the Blessed One?" 62. Jesus said, "I am; and
> 'you will see the Son of Man
> seated at the right hand of the Power,'
> and 'coming with the clouds of heaven.'"

Jesus does not claim to be the Messiah but only admits it after a direct question, which even had to be repeated. We should perhaps remember from my introduction that, if asked by a Gentile, a Jew was bound to admit he was Jewish. Perhaps Jesus felt similarly bound to admit he was the Messiah. In any event Jesus goes on to speak of himself in the highest terms as the Son of Man.

Jesus admits to being the Messiah but shows a decided lack of enthusiasm. He does not state what he as Messiah will do. In contrast, he revels in his description as the Son of Man and glories in what he will do. This is so even though he accepts—with apparent pride—that the Son of Man will suffer. What is the explanation for this indifference to his Messiahship? It cannot be that he has doubts that he is that figure. There is no trace of that. Nor is it that for him the terms *Messiah* and *Son of Man* are synonyms. He treats the notions so differently. The only explanation is that for him to be the Messiah is unimportant compared with being the Son of Man. To be the Messiah may coincide with being the Son of Man, but it is incidental to it.

Jesus' admissions are in response to the eagerness of others to know whether he was the Messiah. They regard the matter as important in a way that he does not. The Messiah in popular conception had some particular attributes, but these are not Jesus' concern. Above all, the Messiah was expected to destroy the dominating foreign power and free the land. At the time of Jesus this foreign power was the Romans. Jesus had no interest in getting rid of them. There is not the slightest sign in any of the Gospels of any hostility on Jesus' part toward the Romans. There is no apparent enmity by Romans toward Jesus until the time of his trial before Pontius Pilate. Roman soldiers did not even form part of the arresting party except in John 18.3. That trial was forced on Pilate by the leading Jews: even then, he showed a remarkable reluctance to execute Jesus.

But at least some of Jesus' disciples thought he was, and wanted him to be, the Messiah. This belief continued after the disciples thought they had witnessed his resurrection. Thus, at the beginning of Acts the risen Jesus is with his disciples:

> 1.6. So when they had come together, they asked him, "Lord, is this the time when you will restore the kingdom to Israel?" 7. He replied, "It is not for you to know the times or periods that the Father has set by his own authority."

The verses are the subject of much controversy, but I find them clear. The disciples ask if the time has come for Jesus "to restore the kingdom to Israel." Restoration cannot refer to a heavenly kingdom that the Jews had not had before; instead, it must refer to the earthly kingdom that the Jews once had but now have lost to the Romans. The disciples are asking if Jesus will now drive out the Romans and return the Jews "to Israel."[4] The two main attributes of the Messiah as a political figure were that he would drive out the foreign oppressor and return the Jews from the diaspora. More to the point is Stephen's defense speech. He was tried before the Sanhedrin for claiming that Jesus would destroy the Temple and change the law of Moses (Acts 6.11ff.). His defense was in the familiar genre of those that do not deny the accuracy of the charges but claim that the real issues are other. The express logic of Stephen's speech is that the lot of the Israelites has been to disobey God and the leaders he appointed and to suffer exile and foreign domination; the Jews are still unrighteous and slew John the Baptist who foretold Jesus and they betrayed and murdered him (Acts 7.1ff.). The unexpressed logic is that the Jews' lack of repentance prevents the return of the Messiah, Jesus, who would drive out the Romans and restore Israel to the Jews.[5] But Jesus did not share that concern of Stephen and of the disciples.[6]

10

✠

JESUS
AND THE
SON
OF MAN

✠ ✠ ✠

I ARGUED IN CHAPTER 5 THAT THERE IS IN MARK A PATTERN of escalation in Jesus' hostility toward the law, especially as seen by the Pharisees. Another pattern exists in Mark with Jesus' description, and therefore Jesus' understanding, of himself. He never designates himself as the Messiah, but fourteen times he calls himself the Son of Man. No one else in Mark uses that term for him. What he meant by the title appears from Mark 8.38:

> Those who are ashamed of me and of my words in this adulterous and sinful generation, of them the Son of Man will also be ashamed when he comes in the glory of his Father with the holy angels.

The Son of Man for Jesus is the Son of God, and that is how he sees himself.[1]

The first part of the pattern is that, of the fourteen times Jesus calls himself the Son of Man, ten are in private to his disciples;

only four are public. These four are the first two, then the one just quoted, and the final one after Jesus has admitted to the high priest that he is the Messiah. In contrast to his revelations to the disciples, in none of these four public instances does Jesus claim that he will suffer.

In Mark 1 Jesus acts as one who believes he is beyond the law. But he is carefully nonconfrontational. That changes in chapter 2. People brought a paralytic to Jesus through the roof of the house where he was.

> 2.5. When Jesus saw their faith, he said to the paralytic, "Son, your sins are forgiven." 6. Now some of the scribes were sitting there, questioning in their hearts, 7. "Why does this fellow speak in this way? It is blasphemy! Who can forgive sins but God alone?" 8. At once Jesus perceived in his spirit that they were discussing these questions among themselves; and he said to them, "Why do you raise such questions in your hearts? 9. Which is easier, to say to the paralytic, 'Your sins are forgiven,' or to say, 'Stand up and take your mat and walk'? 10. But so that you may know that the Son of Man has authority on earth to forgive sins"—he said to the paralytic—11. "I say to you, stand up, take your mat and go to your home." 12. And he stood up, and immediately took the mat and went out before all of them; so that they were all amazed and glorified God, saying, "We have never seen anything like this!"

Jesus begins the confrontation, not the scribes. They think in their hearts but do not say[2] that Jesus blasphemes when he says, "Your sins are forgiven." He is at least claiming to know the mind of God. But then he goes further (Mark 2.10) and claims that the Son of Man—himself, and in the context no other understanding is possible—has authority to forgive sin. With these words and this designation of himself, Jesus greatly escalates the confrontation he has already begun. In no way can it properly be argued that Jesus uses the title "Son of Man" simply to indicate a human being.

In the same chapter, in another confrontation with the Pharisees Jesus willfully defends his disciples for plucking grain on the Sabbath, concluding with this:

> 2.27. Then he said to them, "The sabbath was made for humankind, and not humankind for the sabbath; 28. so the Son of Man is lord even of the sabbath."

Jesus, in the guise of the Son of Man, claims to be lord even of the Sabbath. Few claims of authority could be more striking to Jews. To those who did not accept Jesus' authority, few claims could be more outrageous. It is noteworthy that these first declarations that he is the Son of Man are made by Jesus at the point of his earliest confrontations with the Pharisees.

Then for a time there is silence on Jesus' part on this issue. After Jesus had thoroughly offended the Pharisees by his attitude to the law, after John had been beheaded, after Jesus had performed miracle after miracle, and immediately after his admission to his disciples at Caesarea Phillippi that he was the Messiah, the issue surfaced again. Jesus is still with his disciples.

> 8.31. Then he began to teach them that the Son of Man must undergo great suffering, and be rejected by the elders, the chief priests, and the scribes, and be killed, and after three days rise again. 32. He said all this quite openly. And Peter took him aside and began to rebuke him. 33. But turning and looking at his disciples, he rebuked Peter and said, "Get behind me, Satan! For you are setting your mind not on divine things but on human things."

The episode records a crucial moment in Jesus' life. For the first time he states that he will greatly suffer, be rejected by the Jewish leaders, and be put to death. We know the importance of the moment from the emphasis in Mark: Jesus declared this openly, Peter rebuked him, and Jesus was furious, even calling Peter "Satan."

Peter was astonished and very upset. No wonder. Jesus had just admitted he was the Messiah. Now he was claiming he would be rejected by the Jewish leadership and executed. This was not the traditional understanding of the Messiah. Jesus had come to a new understanding. Near the beginning of his ministry Jesus publicly claimed great things for himself. Then he silenced himself on the issue and concentrated on his teaching and his healing miracles. He had greatly offended the Pharisees by his stance on their understanding of the law. Now he recognizes that his belief in who he is will never be acceptable to the Jewish leadership. To this point he has not extended his hostility to the Temple or to the Sadducees. That is to come, with the so-called cleansing of the Temple.

But to Peter, Jesus is going further: "For you do not mind the things of God but the things of men." What can this mean? In what sense is Peter who rebukes Jesus because he spoke of his sufferings setting his mind on human things? Clearly, Jesus' anger is because Peter has failed to understand. But in what way? I give my explanation in the next chapter.

This private declaration of Jesus to his disciples comes shortly after he refused to give a sign to the Pharisees (Mark 8.11ff.), told his disciples to beware of the yeast of the Pharisees and of Herod (Mark 8.14ff.), and cured the blind man at Bethsaida, sending him home and telling him not even to go into his village (Mark 8.22ff.). Jesus was clearly very frustrated.

Indeed, immediately after this private episode comes Jesus' third public declaration that he is the Son of Man:

8.34. He called the crowd with his disciples, and said to them, "If any want to become my followers, let them deny themselves and take up their cross and follow me. 35. For those who want to save their life will lose it, and those who lose their life for my sake, and for the sake of the gospel, will save it. 36. For what will it profit them to gain the whole world and forfeit their life? 37. Indeed, what can they give in return for their life? 38. Those who are ashamed of me and of my words in this adulterous and sinful generation, of them the Son of Man will also be ashamed when he comes in the glory of his Father with the holy angels."

Here is a direct appeal to the people to follow him. But it is also much more; it is a challenge and a threat. Those who follow him will lose their lives: Jesus is challenging his audience, but he is also challenging the Jewish authorities. Those who do not follow him will be abandoned by Jesus, the Son of Man, when he comes in the glory of God. This moment and what has just gone before are decisive in Jesus' life. Jesus is also making his supreme claim.

Then occur various occasions when Jesus describes himself to his disciples as the "Son of Man." The term is used always in the context of his suffering and betrayal, or his authority, or both (Mark 9.9, 12, 31; 10.33, 45; 14.21, 41).

Jesus' final declaration that he is the Son of Man is at his trial. After admitting to the high priest that he is the Messiah, he warns that he will "see the Son of Man seated at the right hand of the Power and coming with the clouds of heaven." Again the declaration is public and triumphant.

In Mark Jesus is certainly the Messiah, but he never so designates himself. Instead, he calls himself the Son of Man by which he means Son of God. When Jesus first becomes confrontational with the Pharisees, he twice so calls himself the Son of Man in the context of claiming extraordinary power and authority. Then there is a hiatus in the use of the term and Jesus teaches, works miracles, and further affronts the Pharisees. To a question from Peter he admits that he is the Messiah, and he immediately calls himself the Son of Man but in the context of his great suffering, rejection, and death. Jesus has recognized that he has won the undying hatred of the Jewish leadership. He then publicly challenges the crowd to follow him and suffer for his sake or they will meet the vengeance of the Son of Man. Several times he calls himself the Son of Man to his disciples in the twin contexts of his suffering and authority. Finally, triumphantly, on trial for his life, he publicly proclaims himself the Son of Man. Because of this very precise usage of the term, I would reject suggestions such as those of Geza Vermes[3] that Jesus uses "Son of Man" just to mean something like "I."

The term "Son of Man" appears frequently in the Old Testament, but seems to have no precise theological meaning. It may mean "man" or "human being."[4] When Jesus refers to himself as the Son of Man before the high priest, he quotes Daniel 7.13. The passage reads:

> As I watched in the night visions, I saw one like the Son of Man[5] coming with the clouds of heaven. And he came to the Ancient One and was presented before him. 14. To him was given dominion and glory and kingship, that all peoples, nations, and languages should serve him. His dominion is an everlasting dominion that shall not pass away, and his kingship is one that shall never be destroyed.

What Daniel meant by "Son of Man" is a matter of dispute,[6] but it is of little concern to us. What matters for us is not any original intent of the prophet but what Jesus meant and what the high priest understood. We know that Jesus used "Son of Man" to mean himself as the Son of God, and it is reasonable to assume that Daniel 7.14, which Jesus does not quote (he has no need to), was in the forefront of his mind. Jesus was proclaiming his future glory and everlasting kingship over all peoples. The high priest, too, would know what Jesus meant, and he wrongfully tore his robes. Previously I believed that he said Jesus had blasphemed when he admitted to being the Messiah. Now I see the blasphemy to reside rather in the claim that Jesus would see himself at the right hand of God and in the implicit claim that Jesus would be the everlasting king. We can now understand why Pilate asked Jesus, "Are you the king of the Jews?" Jesus' claim to be king does not otherwise emerge. It is also perhaps significant that in Matthew 26.63 Jesus does not admit to being the Messiah, but after he quotes Daniel (Matthew 26.64), the high priest tears his clothes and says, "He has blasphemed!" (26.65). Again Pilate asks, "Are you the king of the Jews?" (27.11).[7]

In Matthew Jesus calls himself the Son of Man more than twice as often as he does in Mark. The uses are much as in Mark, but there is some loss of the structure. At Matthew 8.20 he tells a scribe that "the Son of Man has nowhere to lay his head,"[8] thus revealing his suffering as the Son of Man to an outsider. Still, this scribe did want to follow Jesus. The term in Matthew 11.19 fits nowhere in the pattern observed for Mark: Jesus said, "The Son of Man came eating and drinking, and they say, 'Look, a glutton and a drunkard, a friend of tax collectors and sinners.'"[9] Luke, who calls Jesus the Son of Man twenty-five times, is much like Mark. But he has the women who visited the empty tomb say, "Remember how he told you, while he was still in Galilee, that the Son of Man must be handed over to sinners, and be crucified, and on the third day rise again" (Luke 24.6). So in Luke others, echoing Jesus, also call him the "Son of Man." Still, the women are citing Jesus' name for himself.

11

·**I**·

JESUS
AS
OTHERS
SAW HIM

✠ ✠ ✠

For Jesus, baptism by John the Baptist was a cathartic experience. It drove him into the wilderness for reflection for forty days, a period not to be taken literally but recalling the forty years' exile of the Jews in the desert. When John was arrested, Jesus returned to Galilee and preached John's message of repentance but with a difference: Jesus claimed that the time was now fulfilled and that the kingdom of God was at hand. Jesus had come to believe that he was the Son of God. He also believed he was the Messiah, but that was incidental to his larger claim, and he had no interest in secular politics.

But how did others see him? We already have part of the answer. The Romans did not regard him as a threat. We have no information on their attitude, and that in itself is significant. No doubt they kept him under observation, but we are not told. Of course, so long as he was in Galilee he was not in territory that was directly under Roman control. So little was he regarded as a threat that even after his crucifixion the Romans did not pursue his followers, not even—let me stress—when the disciples continued to believe Jesus was the political Messiah (Acts 1.6), not even when Peter and John preached him as such. The first Christian martyr, Stephen, was tried, arrested, and killed by the Jews, not by the Romans (Acts 6.12–8.1). In contrast, the supporters of Herod Antipas were hostile toward Jesus. This can be no surprise. They regarded John the Baptist and his teaching as dangerous, and John was arrested and eventually put to death. Jesus had been baptized by John and was continuing John's message but with greater urgency. Jesus' call for repentance, like John's, was seen as a political threat because there was a notable public sinner in Herod himself. John, indeed, had expressly singled Herod out for fierce criticism.

The Pharisees, who were those most interested in leading the good Jewish life, were like others hoping for and expecting the Messiah. We may assume that John's call for repentance heightened this expectation. They were intrigued by Jesus' miracles, and the fundamental question for them was whether Jesus was the Messiah. They followed Jesus about to find out what kind of a person he was. Jesus became ever more confrontational with them. From his disrespect—as they saw it—for the law and his lack of knowledge of, and skill with, the law they decided he was not the Messiah.

Jesus gathered around him immediate followers, the disciples. Who did they think he was? The short answer is the Messiah (Mark 8.29).[1] At that, they believed he was the political Messiah who would drive out the foreign dominating power and restore the kingdom to Israel. This understanding of Jesus continued after his crucifixion when the disciples were convinced he had risen from the dead (Acts 1.6). The disciples' belief that Jesus was the political Messiah and his disinterest in the issue explain puzzling features in their relationship. Thus, it is emphasized again and again that the disciples did not understand Jesus' message. Of course not! They were looking for something else. Likewise, they displayed a remarkable lack of interest in Jesus' miracles. The explanation is that they did not see these as geared to the political cause. Miracles of individual healing, exorcisms, and miracles controlling nature were not regarded as traits of the Messiah.

Jesus proclaimed that the kingdom of God was at hand and recruited his first disciples (Mark 1.16ff.) before he had (to our knowledge) performed any miracle. It may be remembered that John the Baptist had disciples but is not credited with miracles. Miracles are not a necessary part of the message of repentance and of the kingdom of God. Jesus told Simon and Peter to follow him and he would make them fish for men (Mark 1.17), a nicely ambiguous claim. In what sense would they capture people? In Capernaum on the Sabbath Jesus taught with authority—that is, like a rabbi[2]—but we are not told what he taught (Mark 1.21ff.). He exorcised an unclean spirit, and those present then asked themselves: "What is this? A new teaching—with authority! He commands even the unclean spirits, and they obey him." The exorcism is regarded as part of Jesus' teaching, and it causes amazement. The disciples' reaction is not noted. Jesus then performs various miracles, but we are not told the effect they had upon the disciples.

From those who followed him he selected twelve whom he also named apostles (Mark 3.14). Twelve is a symbolic number to represent the twelve tribes of Israel. The twelve apostles are named differently in the different lists (Mark 3.16ff.; Matthew 10.1ff.; Luke 6.12ff.; John 6.67ff., 20.24),[3] and probably they should be seen as a fluctuating group. To these favored few, Jesus gave the power of exorcism (Mark 3.15). Jesus taught in parables. After the parable of the sower and the seed, those who were around him "along with the twelve" asked him about it (4.10). The point to notice is that the disciples, too, do not understand the parable. Indeed, he explains it to them (4.13ff.). He taught in other parables and then:

> Mark 4.33. With many such parables he spoke the word to them [i.e., the crowd], as they were able to hear it; 34. he did not speak to them except in parables, but he explained everything in private to his disciples.

Jesus, as I have said before, appears to intend to be incomprehensible. In fact, he is so incomprehensible that not even his disciples could understand him.

Following on this is one of the few episodes where the disciples seem impressed by a miracle: it concerns them (4.35ff.). They were crossing the sea in a boat, a great storm arose, and they were afraid they would be swamped. They woke Jesus in fear:

> 4.39. He woke up and rebuked the wind, and said to the sea, "Peace! Be still!" Then the wind ceased, and there was a dead calm. 40. He said to them, "Why are you afraid? Have you still no faith?" 41. And they were filled with great awe and said to one another, "Who then is this, that even the wind and the sea obey him?"

Jesus treated their panic as absence of faith in him—in fact, a lack of understanding. "They said ($\check{\epsilon}\lambda\epsilon\gamma o\nu$) to one another" is in the imperfect tense: "they said repeatedly." Why is their astonishment that Jesus could control a storm stressed, and this in the context of their absence of faith, when we are not told of any reaction to other miracles? No convincing explanation seems readily to be found. I would suggest that it is because they saw Jesus controlling nature, something they did not expect. The standard traditions did not portray God as giving the Messiah control over nature. Jesus rebuked them for their lack of faith because they still did not see him as he believed he was.

More miracles followed, and Jesus sent out his disciples: they called for repentance, cast out many demons, and cured the sick (6.7ff.). Their reaction to their own powers is not stated. This contrast is striking—no mention of reaction to their own miracles, none usually to those of Jesus, but sharp reaction to Jesus' miracle in the boat. It becomes even more so when the boat episode occurs again at Mark 6.47ff. I argued in chapter 1 that these two episodes and one in Mark 8.1ff. have the same origin. This time, when Jesus walked on water they were terrified and astonished, "for they did not understand about the loaves, but their hearts were hardened" (6.52). Why does Mark tell us that their hearts were hardened? And what does it mean that they did not understand about the loaves? Some present-day theologians say that the disciples did not see the Eucharistic symbolism of the multiplication of the loaves. But that is to look at the episode with modern eyes. What we have to do is something different. The issue is not how should the episode be understood by modern theologians but what it meant to Mark. (I need scarcely add that seeing the episode as involving "the Messiah presiding at the messianic banquet" is far-fetched in the extreme—there is no talk of this bread being the messianic body.) The nucleus of the solution is suggested by Daniel J. Harrington: The disciples had not gone beyond seeing Jesus as the Messiah to understand that Jesus was more, the Son of God.[4] It is in this sense that "their hearts were hardened." For them, the miracle of feeding a multitude with bread was no indication of the political Messiah. They could not understand why he had acted as he did. This is why in the previous version at Mark 4.40 (which, however, does not contain the miracle of the loaves), Jesus asked, "Have you still no faith?" He was not asking if they had no faith in him as the Messiah. If they had not, they would not have been his disciples.[5] The boat episode appears a third time at Mark 8.14ff., which does not involve a miracle:

Now the disciples had forgotten to bring any bread; and they had only one loaf with them in the boat. 15. And he cautioned them, saying, "Watch out—beware of the yeast of the Pharisees and the yeast of Herod." 16. They said to one another, "It is because we have no bread." 17. And becoming aware of it, Jesus said to them, "Why are you talking about having no bread? Do you still not perceive or understand? Are your hearts hardened? 18. Do you have eyes, and fail to see? Do you have ears, and fail to hear? And do you not remember? 19. When I broke the five loaves for the five thousand, how many baskets full of broken pieces did you collect?" They said to him, "Twelve." 20. "And the seven for the four thousand, how many baskets full of broken pieces did you collect?" And they said to him, "Seven." 21. Then he said to them, "Do you not yet understand?"

The emphasis is again on the disciples' failure to understand the miracle. I suggest that they could not understand because they were looking for something different: they wanted and expected Jesus to be the political Messiah.

This approach is greatly strengthened by a detail in Mark 8. Immediately after the feeding of the multitude and before the boat episode, Pharisees asked for a sign from heaven (8.11ff.). But Jesus had just performed a miracle. This for the Pharisees was not enough. It was not the right sort of miracle. The Pharisees were looking for a sign of a very different nature. The Pharisees wished to know if Jesus was the Messiah. His irrelevant (to them) miracles were not enough, and they wanted a sign from heaven.[6]

(There is much more to the episode that also is not easily understandable to modern commentators.[7] We are told there was only one loaf in the boat, but this is used only as a lead-in to Jesus' warning, "Watch out—beware of the yeast of the Pharisees and the yeast of Herod." What can this reference to yeast mean? What is this yeast, and why should the disciples beware of it? Understandably on one level, but clearly wrongly, the disciples think Jesus is rebuking them for not bringing bread. To enlighten the disciples, Jesus reminds them of the miracles of the loaves and fishes. He emphasizes the amount that was left over: the stress is on his ability to provide superabundance. He contrasts his leaven with the leaven of the Pharisees and of Herod. What is that leaven? I suggest that for Jesus here the leaven of the Pharisees was overabundance of interpretation that obscured God's purpose in the law. Herod's leaven was overexercising his power: for instance, to marry incestuously and to execute the innocent John.)

Stress continues on the disciples' lack of comprehension (Mark 7.17). They did not understand his saying that whatever goes into a person cannot defile. What was it to them that no food was unclean? Indeed, Jesus' teaching, unless it was restricted as I suggested in chapter 6, would seem to them to be directly contrary to God's command.

Jesus performed other miracles. He cast out the demon from the daughter of the Gentile woman (7.24ff.); he cured the man who was deaf and dumb (7.31); he made the blind man see (8.22ff.). Never are we told of the disciples' reactions.[8] Then Jesus asked them who he was, and Peter replied, "You are the Messiah" (8.29). This is followed as we saw in chapter 10 by Jesus saying the Son of Man must suffer, Peter rebuking him, and Jesus calling Peter "Satan."

There remains to be mentioned the greatest obstacle to the disciples' understanding Jesus. Judaism is fundamentally and obstinately monotheistic. That conception has no place for a Son of God with divine status, in fact, a second God. Indeed, so far was the notion of a second God removed from Jewish comprehension that at Jesus' trial the high priest did not ask whether he claimed to be divine but whether he claimed to be the Messiah. Likewise, after the resurrection, in the first chapter of Acts, the disciples thought Jesus was the Messiah, not God, and that, too, was emphatically Stephen's stance.

The disciples' failure to understand was great. They saw Jesus as the Messiah and not as anything greater. This explains their lack of interest in his miracles—the wrong kind—and their bewilderment at his teaching. It is this which explains Jesus' rebuke to Peter that his mind is on earthly things. It is this which explains why they deserted him when he was arrested (14.50). Jesus seemed a failure, not the Messiah. Peter hung around during the night session of the Sanhedrin, but his faith was so weakened that he denied Jesus three times (14.66ff.). The disciples do not appear again during Jesus' lifetime, not even at his execution. This cannot be a surprise. From their perspective Jesus had let them down. He was not the Messiah.

From the very beginning of his ministry Jesus attracted crowds who are to be regarded as neither Pharisees nor disciples. They were astounded by his teaching (1.21ff.), but this was in the context of his act of exorcism. What was it about Jesus that interested them? The basic answer is his exorcisms and his miracles. Their amazement is stressed (1.27, 2.12, 5.42, 7.37). But they could not explain his conduct. Indeed, they thought he was insane (3.21, 31ff.), as did his own family. The people did not understand his teaching (4.1ff.), which is not surprising because he intended not to be understood (4.10ff., 33f.). In the country of the Gerasenes (5.1ff.) he cast out the legion of devils, and when they entered pigs who rushed into the sea, the people were so terrified that they asked Jesus to leave the neighborhood (5.17). Still, Jesus continued to attract attention, and large crowds followed him as we are continually told (5.24; 6.33ff., 53f.; 7.14ff., 31ff.; 8.1, 34ff.; 9.14, 25; 10.1).

But gradually—the first sign is as late as Mark 10.13ff.—Jesus began to win popular approval. People brought little children that he might touch them. The context does not indicate that the children were sick, and the disciples' response and Jesus' reaction would seem to indicate that sickness was not an issue. The feeling seems rather to be that Jesus' touching a child would have a great impact on the child's life. We cannot be more precise. But immediately after this episode we are told (10.17ff.) that a man rushed up and knelt before him and asked, "Good teacher, what must I do to inherit eternal life?" Jesus was coming to be regarded not just as a miracle worker but as good and as a teacher and, at that, one of religious significance who could show the way to salvation. Only when Jesus was approaching Jerusalem did he receive a tumultuous welcome from the crowd, which regarded him as a religious leader:

> Mark 11.8. Many people spread their cloaks on the road, and others spread leafy branches that they had cut in the fields.
> 9. Then those who went ahead and those who followed were shouting,
> > "Hosanna!
> > Blessed is the one who comes in
> > the name of the Lord!
> > Blessed is the coming kingdom
> > of our ancestor David!"

The precise meaning of the acclamation is unclear. *Hosanna* is usually regarded as a transliteration of the Aramaic word whose Hebrew equivalent is in Psalm 118.25. Literally, it means "help now" or "save now." In that sense it is used in addressing kings at 2 Samuel 14.4 and 2 Kings 6.26. But Psalms 113–18 were used together liturgically in synagogues on joyous festivals, and in this connection these Psalms were designated "Hallel." In this context the word *hosanna* would be known to everyone but would be used as an acclamation of joy, even as a greeting to a famous rabbi or pilgrims.[9] In its entirety Psalm 118 is a thanksgiving to God for deliverance in battle. Mark's "Blessed is the one that comes in the name of the Lord" is an exact translation of part of Psalm 118.26, which continues, "We bless you from the house of the Lord." It is therefore a salutation or blessing to a pilgrim or rabbi who comes from outside and is uttered by those already in place. It is as a teacher or leader from afar that Jesus is welcomed by those of that place. In view of the Psalm's use at joyous festivals in general, it is doubtful whether its original nature as thanksgiving for delivery in battle should be stressed. The cry that follows in Mark, "Blessed is the coming kingdom of our father, David," is of obscure meaning. Mark does not trace Jesus' lineage. It is those who utter the cry who call David their father, and David is otherwise called "our father" only in Acts 4.25, where the precise intent is obscure. Besides, Bar Berakh 166 says that the word *fathers* was used only of Abraham, Isaac, and Jacob.[10] Jesus' response to the notion of a king descended from David is set out in my chapter 1.[11]

The acclamation is joyous and overwhelming: Jesus has at last the acceptance of the crowd. But immediately thereafter occurred the so-called cleansing of the Temple (Mark 11.15ff.), which must have been regarded as a terrible affront by many of the ordinary people. Still we are not directly told anything about their reaction. We read only that the chief priests and scribes looked for a way to kill him because all the crowd was spellbound by his teaching (11.18). So the leaders at least thought Jesus had retained support. Subsequently, Jesus taught that the Messiah would not be the son of David, and the crowd rejoiced (12.35ff.). The crowd believed that Jesus was revealing himself as the Messiah.

But then Jesus was arrested, tried by the Sanhedrin, and tried again by Pontius Pilate. Pilate offered to release Jesus, but the crowd shouted insistently that he should crucify him. Clearly Jesus had lost the crowd's support, whether these were different people (because those who supported him had melted away), or the people were offended by Jesus' behavior in cleansing the Temple, or they had been incited by the Jewish leadership. In any event, this crowd did not believe at this stage that Jesus was the Messiah. And we are not told of any who still did.

12
✠
JESUS
AND
ISAIAH
✠ ✠ ✠

THERE ARE RESEMBLANCES BETWEEN ISAIAH AND JESUS THAT are too close to be coincidental. It would be going too far to suggest that Jesus deliberately modeled himself on Isaiah: Jesus did not think of himself as anyone's follower, and he would feel no need of Isaiah's authority. Besides, for Isaiah, the deliverer of Israel seems to be a descendant of David (Isaiah 9.7). Jesus did not regard himself as descended from David (Mark 12.35ff.) but directly from God (Mark 1.11; 2.10, 28; 3.11f.). Still, no one, I hope, will deny the parallelisms. At the very least, Jesus has been profoundly influenced by Isaiah. But once one has seen the similarities, it is the very differences that loom large in significance.

Isaiah, like Jesus, stresses the corruption of Israel and its neglect of God. This appears from the outset of the prophet's book. God reared the children and brought them up, but they rebelled against him. The sinful nation is laden with iniquity; the people have despised God and are wholly estranged (1.2ff.). Isaiah makes God ask the people: "Why do you seek further beatings, why do you continue to rebel?" (1.5). There is in this almost a plea that the people repent because God wants not to have to punish them.[1] In fact, there is an expressed optimism in Isaiah, which I find lacking in Jesus, that the people will repent and be saved:

> Isaiah 1.18. Come now, let us argue it out,
>   says the Lord:
>   though your sins are like scarlet,
>   they shall be like snow;
>   though they are red like crimson,
>   they shall become like wool.
>   19. If you are willing and obedient,
>   you shall eat the good of the land;
>   20. but if you refuse and rebel,
>   you shall be devoured by the sword;
>   for the mouth of the Lord has spoken.[2]

Isaiah adds, "But rebels and sinners shall be destroyed together, and those who forsake the Lord shall be consumed" (1.28). Isaiah seems to reserve this fate for the wicked, whereas for Jesus the awful days of God's vengeance fall on the sinner and innocent alike (Mark 13.14ff.). "Woe to those who are pregnant and to those who are nursing infants in those days. Pray that it may not be in winter" (Mark 13.17ff.). Certainly some will be saved because God will cut short these days for the sake of the elect (13.20), but clearly for Jesus the elect will also suffer.

Isaiah's God is hostile toward sacrifices, even of grain:

> Isaiah 66.3. Whoever slaughters an ox is like
>   one who kills a human being;
>   whoever sacrifices a lamb, like
>   one who breaks a dog's neck;
>   whoever presents a grain offering,
>   like one who offers swine's blood;

> whoever makes a memorial offering of
> frankincense, like one who blesses
> an idol.
> These have chosen their own ways,
> and in their abominations they take delight.

Isaiah 1.11.
> What to me is the multitude of
> your sacrifices?
> says the Lord;
> I have had enough of burnt
> offerings of rams
> and the fat of fed beasts;
> I do not delight in the blood
> of bulls,
> or of lambs, or of goats.

12.
> When you come to appear
> before me,
> who asked this from your hand?
> Trample my courts no more;

13.
> bringing offerings is futile;
> incense is an abomination to me.

But as the context of the second passage especially makes clear, God's hostility is not so much toward the sacrifice itself as toward its uselessness, and it is worse in the absence of the proper spirit of piety and respect. Isaiah, of course, did not stand alone in showing God as hostile toward Jewish festivals and sacrifices in the absence of repentance.[3] Amos 5.21ff. is especially noteworthy:

> I hate, I despise your festivals,
> and I take no delight in your solemn
> assemblies.

22.
> Even though you offer me your
> burnt offerings and grain offerings,

I will not accept them;
and the offerings of well-being of
your fatted animals
I will not look upon.
23. Take away from me the noise of your songs;
I will not listen to the melody of your harps.
24. But let justice roll down like waters,
and righteousness like an ever-
flowing stream.

Jesus went much further than Isaiah in the so-called cleansing of the Temple: he physically inhibited the performance of the sacrifices (Mark 11.15ff.). And those affected would be the good and bad alike. Still, Isaiah's God declared the Temple unnecessary, perhaps even wicked:

Isaiah 66.1. Thus says the Lord:
Heaven is my throne
and the earth is my footstool;
what is the house that you would
build for me,
and what is my resting place?
2. All these things my hand has
made,
and so all these things
are mine,
says the Lord.

We should see Jesus' obstruction of the payment of the Temple tax and the performance of sacrifice as a less sophisticated form of Isaiah's protest.

Isaiah objected to the observance of the Sabbath and festivals

(Isaiah 1.13f.). This is again in the context of Israel's outward observance in the absence of true repentance. We have seen time and time again Jesus' opposition to the strict Pharisaic attitude toward the Sabbath.

Seen against the background of Isaiah, Jesus' behavior in cleansing the Temple—an act essentially hostile toward traditional Jewish worship   becomes more comprehensible.[4]

Jesus' prophecy that the Temple would be destroyed seems to be a deliberate reference to the arrogance of the Israelites in Isaiah 9.8ff.:

> The Lord sent a word against
>   Jacob,
>   and it fell on Israel;
> 9. and all the people knew it—
>   Ephraim and the inhabitants of
>   Samaria—
>   but in pride and arrogance of
>   heart they said:
> 10. "The bricks have fallen,
>   but we will build with dressed
>   stones;
>   the sycamores have been cut
>   down,
>   but we will put cedars in their
>   place."

The emphasis on the "dressed stones" in Isaiah is repeated for Jesus in Mark 13.1ff., with "'Look, teacher, what large stones and what large buildings!' Then Jesus asked him, 'Do you see these great buildings? Not one stone will be left here upon another; all will be thrown down.'"[5] In Isaiah the implication is that the dressed stones will fall, just as the bricks fell. The prophesy in Isaiah is about the destruction of a replacement building that will be constructed. Jesus' prophesy is about the destruction of the second Temple, also a replacement building—the first Temple was destroyed in 63 B.C.—that was under construction.

Like Jesus (Mark 5.22ff.), Isaiah's God seems not to be troubled by female uncleanliness: he is depicted both as a woman giving birth (Isaiah 42.14) and as a midwife (Isaiah 66.9) who becomes unclean by contact. But here there is another significant point of difference. Isaiah rails against coquettishness in a way that to modern eyes looks sexist:

> 3.16. The Lord said:
>   Because the daughters of Zion are haughty
>   and walk with outstretched necks,
>   glancing wantonly with their eyes,
>   mincing along as they go,
>   tinkling with their feet;
> 17. the Lord will afflict with scabs
>   the heads of the daughters of Zion,
>   and the Lord will lay bare their secret parts.

18. In that day the Lord will take away the finery of the anklets, the headbands, and the crescents; 19. the pendants, the bracelets, and the scarfs; 20. the headdresses, the armlets, the sashes, the perfume boxes, and the amulets; 21. the signet rings and nose rings; 22. the festal robes, the mantles, the cloaks, and the handbags; 23. the garments of gauze, the linen garments, the turbans, and the veils.

> 24. Instead of perfume there will be a stench;
>   and instead of a sash, a rope;
>   and instead of a well-set hair, baldness;

and instead of a rich robe, a binding
of sackcloth;
instead of beauty, shame.

The passage is the only one in which Isaiah rails against women,
but it is long, has ugly sexual overtures, and is extreme. In contrast,
Jesus seems to have been sexually attractive to women and to
have enjoyed the fact. There is an obvious erotic element in the
woman's anointing Jesus' head with precious ointment, and he
took evident pleasure in her behavior (Mark 14.3ff.). Women followed him to Jerusalem and were even present at his crucifixion—
as were Mary Magdalene, Mary the mother of James the younger,
and Salome—when his male followers had disappeared (Mark
15.40f.). Indeed, the women are described as "many." Jesus was
beguiled by the Syrophoenician Gentile woman into curing her
daughter, who had an unclean spirit (Mark 7.24ff.).

Totally lacking from Jesus is Isaiah's prophecy that aliens will
devour the land of Israel (Isaiah 1.7; 10.1ff.) but that Israel will sur-
vive (14.1ff.), Jerusalem will arise (52.1ff.), and God will bring
back the dispersed to Israel (11.11ff.). I have insisted that, although
Jesus believed he was the Messiah, he was indifferent to the
Messiah's traditional role of driving out the foreign occupiers of
Israel and returning the dispersed. Not even his reliance on Isaiah
influenced him on this. Jesus' picture of himself as doomed to suffer owes much to Isaiah 53.

The most significant similarity and difference between Isaiah
and Jesus is the deliberate obscurity in the message they present:

Isaiah 6.8. Then I heard the voice of the Lord saying,
"Whom shall I send, and who will go for us?" And I said,
"Here am I; send me!" 9. And he said, "Go and say to this
people:

'Keep listening, but do not comprehend;
keep looking, but do not understand.'
10. Make the mind of this people dull,
and stop their ears,
and shut their eyes,
so that they may not look with their eyes,
and listen with their ears,
and comprehend with their minds,
and turn and be healed."
11. Then I said, "How long,
O Lord?" And he said:
"Until cities lie waste
without inhabitant,
and houses without people,
and the land is utterly desolate;
12. until the Lord sends everyone far away,
and vast is the emptiness in the
midst of the land.
13. Even if a tenth part remain in it,
it will be burned again,
like a terebinth or an oak
whose stump remains standing
when it is felled."
The holy seed is its stump.

Jesus' deliberate obfuscation of which he even boasts must derive
from this. But again the all-important point is the difference in
emphasis. God tells Isaiah that he is to say to the people to keep listening but not understand, to keep looking but not see. The tone
is threatening. God is made to want vengeance. But beneath it all
is the expectation of repentance and the desire that the people will
finally repent. Isaiah is to tell the people they will hear but not

understand. He is not told to speak incomprehensibly, although he is to make the mind of the people dull. The point is to force the people to seek understanding. Indeed, Isaiah's message of the need of repentance is everywhere crystal clear—unlike that of Jesus in Mark. When Jesus claims that he speaks so that people will not understand, he does not put them on notice and he is not seeking their repentance. Otherwise, he would not explain to the disciples alone who likewise have not understood. (It may be noted, although it would scarcely be doubted, that Jesus follows the Hebrew, not the Septuagint, version of Isaiah. The Septuagint has at Isaiah 6.10, "For the heart of this people has become gross, and their ears are dull of hearing, and their eyes have been closed; lest they should see with their eyes, and understand with their heart, and be converted, and I should heal them." In the Septuagint God is taking a less active role in obfuscation. I mention this because the redactor of Acts habitually uses the Septuagint.)

Last among the differences is a charitableness in Isaiah toward the weak and oppressed that is largely absent from Mark's Jesus.

> Isaiah 1.16. Wash yourselves; make yourselves clean;
> remove the evil of your doings from
> before my eyes;
> cease to do evil;
> 17. learn to do good; seek justice,
> rescue the oppressed, defend the orphan,
> plead for the widow.

> Isaiah 32.1. See, a king will reign in righteousness,
> and princes will rule with justice.
> 2. Each will be like a hiding place from the
> wind,
> a covert from the tempest,

like streams of water in a dry place,
like the shade of a great rock in a weary
land.

3. Then the eyes of those who have
sight will not be closed,
and the ears of those who have hearing
will listen.

4. The minds of the rash will have good
judgment,
and the tongues of stammerers will speak
readily and
distinctly.

5. A fool will no longer be called noble,
nor a villain said to be honorable.

Isaiah 35.1. The wilderness and the dry
land shall be glad,
the desert shall rejoice and
blossom;
like the crocus it shall blossom
abundantly,
and rejoice with joy and
singing.
The glory of Lebanon shall be
given to it,
the majesty of Carmel and
Sharon.
They shall see the glory of the
Lord.
the majesty of our God.

3. Strengthen the weak hands,
and make firm the feeble knees.

4. Say to those who are of a fearful
        heart,
    "Be strong, do not fear!
    Here is your God.
        He will come with vengeance,
    with terrible recompense.
        He will come and save you."
5. Then the eyes of the blind shall
        be opened,
    and the ears of the deaf
        unstopped;
6. then the lame shall leap like
        a deer,
    and the tongue of the speechless
        sing for joy.
    For waters shall break forth in the
        wilderness,
    and streams in the desert;
7. the burning sand shall become
        a pool,
    and the thirsty ground springs
        of water;
    the haunt of jackals shall become
        a swamp.
    the grass shall become reeds and
        rushes.

Isaiah 40.1. Comfort, O comfort my people,
        says your God.
        2. Speak tenderly to Jerusalem,
            and cry to her
        that she has served her term,

that her penalty is paid,
that she has received from the
Lord's hand
double for all her sins.[6]

This last text has no equivalent in Mark. Jesus does not prophesy the eventual redemption of the people of Israel.

13

✠

MARK
AND
PROPHECIES

✠　✠　✠

MARK IS STRIKINGLY DIFFERENT FROM THE OTHER GOSPELS
with regard to prophecies about Jesus. Not only are references to
prophecies scarce in Mark but two types are totally absent.[1]

The first type absent from Mark is exemplified by Matthew
1.22f. on the virgin birth:

> "All this took place to fulfill what had been spoken by the
> Lord through the prophet: 23. 'Look, the virgin shall con-
> ceive and bear a son, and they shall name him Emmanuel,'
> which means, 'God is with us.'"

The reference to the prophet is particularly to Isaiah 7.14: "Therefore the Lord himself will give you a sign. Look, the young woman
is with child and shall bear a son, and shall name him Immanuel."
In this type, it would seem that the prophecy existed, and a myth
about Jesus was created to make him its fulfillment.[2] The virgin
birth is absent from Mark.

The second type absent from Mark is exemplified by John 19.23ff.:

> When the soldiers had crucified Jesus, they took his clothes and divided them into four parts, one for each soldier. They also took his tunic; now the tunic was seamless, woven in one piece from the top. 24. So they said to one another, "Let us not tear it, but cast lots for it to see who will get it." This was to fulfill what the Scripture says,
> > "They divided my clothes among themselves.
> > and for my clothing they cast lots."

The reference is to Psalm 22.18. But the Psalm is not offering a prophecy about the Messiah; it is a lament by someone beset by his enemies. In this type an irrelevant piece of Scripture is invoked in order to turn it into a prophecy about Jesus, increasing the credibility of what is attributed to him. Plausibly this Johannine prophecy is created to give additional weight to a striking event that was rooted in tradition. The tradition itself is in Mark 15.24: "They shared out his clothes, casting lots to decide what each should have." But in Mark, quite properly, there is no reference to any prophecy.

It is in fact instructive to go through what may appear to be prophecies in Mark in the order in which they emerge.

Thus, the first appears at Mark 7.6ff. when Jesus rails against the Pharisees and scribes who asked why Jesus' disciples ate without washing their hands:

> He said to them, "Isaiah prophesied rightly about you hypocrites, as it is written,
> > 'This people honors me with their lips,
> > > but their hearts are far from me;
> > 7. in vain do they worship me,

teaching human precepts as doctrines.'
8. You abandon the commandment of God and hold
to human tradition."

The quotation is from Isaiah 29.13. But despite the wording *prophesied* ($\pi\rho o\epsilon\phi\acute{\eta}\tau\epsilon\upsilon\sigma\epsilon\nu$), no prophecy is involved.

The second apparent reference to prophecy is in Mark 9.13: "But I tell you that Elijah has come and they did to him whatever they pleased, as it is written of him." There was a belief that Elijah had to return before the Messiah could appear. Here Jesus was claiming that John the Baptist was Elijah.[3] But there was no tradition that the returned Elijah would suffer and be put to death. The prophecy in "as it is written of him" was nonexistent.

The third prophecy is in Mark 10.32ff.:

They were on the road, going up to Jerusalem, and Jesus was walking ahead of them; they were amazed, and those who followed were afraid. He took the twelve aside again and began to tell them what was to happen to him 33. saying, "See, we are going up to Jerusalem, and the Son of Man will be handed over to the chief priests and the scribes, and they will condemn him to death; then they will hand him over to the Gentiles; 34. they will mock him, and spit upon him, and flog him, and kill him; and after three days he will rise again."[4]

This is a prophecy by Jesus about what will happen to him. It is not a prophecy that exalts the nature of Jesus and that is backed by the authority of Scripture. Even if the words are not to be regarded as written with hindsight, the prediction was not difficult given what Jesus was about to do in the Temple when he arrived in Jerusalem.

The next prophecy concerns the destruction of the Temple:

Mark 13.1. As he came out of the temple, one of his disciples said to him, "Look, Teacher, what large stones and what large buildings!" 2. Then Jesus asked him, "Do you see these great buildings? Not one stone will be left here upon another; all will be thrown down."

In the Gospels Jesus does not predict that he himself will destroy the Temple, although that meaning was attributed to him. This prediction leads on to the prophecy of the great desolation (Mark 13.14ff.), which appears to be founded on Isaiah 1.18ff. In the absence of any time-frame the prediction is uninformative. The issue of timing is vital. Indeed, Peter, James, John, and Andrew had already asked him (Mark 13.4) with respect to the destruction of the Temple, "Tell us, when will this be, and what will be the sign that all these things are about to be accomplished?"

Finally, at the Last Supper Jesus predicted his betrayal by Judas:

Mark 14.21. For the Son of Man goes as it is written of him, but woe to that one by whom the Son of Man is betrayed! It would have been better for that one not to have been born.

But there is no prediction in Scripture that the Messiah would be betrayed, even if the Messiah is to be identified as the suffering servant of God in Isaiah 52.13–53.12. There is here no precision in any reliance on a prophecy from Scripture.

Prophecies in Mark are remarkably unimportant. Jesus' role as Messiah or Son of God is never bolstered by a prophecy based on Scripture. We are never asked in Mark to see Jesus as special because of prophecies about him. The very different use of prophecy in the other Gospels is for me an indication of manipulation and evidence that they belong to a generation subsequent to Mark.

14

✠

JESUS, THE LEADER OF A CULT

✠ ✠ ✠

IN NO WAY DO I USE THE TERM *CULT* PEJORATIVELY. I USE *cult* to denote a form of worship that stresses devotion to a person or god rather than theology and that tends to emphasize initiates who surround the charismatic leader. These charismatic figures have several typical attributes. These include a paradoxical adherence of devotees to the leader in the face of facts that logically should lead to disillusionment. The leaders often report miraculous mystical and conversion experiences that start them on their road to religious leadership. Something akin to supernatural powers is attributed to the leaders. Their teachings tend to be all-embracing with prescriptions for beliefs and daily behavior. The followers have a sense of transcendent significance. They may embody the leaders with an anarchical ego, free from conventional restraint, and be delighted when the leaders outsmart authority

133

figures. The leaders may demonstrate mood swings, sometimes seeming benign and loving, at other times cruel and punishing. They may even instigate an apocalyptic ending to their movement.[1]

I would add that they claim that the only way to salvation is through faith in them. Faith in the leader is essential. He deliberately seeks out immediate followers. The leader separates his followers from their families. The leader performs miracles. He couches his message in high-flown, largely incomprehensible rhetoric. He insists that false prophets will come in his name. In a very deep sense women seem to understand him. The leader grants children a special place. He deliberately challenges institutional authority. He predicts that his followers will be persecuted and even killed because of him. His followers claim they will suffer death rather than desert him. They arm themselves. The leader predicts his enemies will kill him but that this will mark the beginning, not the end.

In this chapter I wish to trace the emergence of Jesus as a cult leader with these attributes. I will not arrange the attributes in order of importance. Rather, I select the order in which they first appear in Mark to see whether any pattern emerges. We have already seen patterns in Mark: first, of escalation of hostility toward the Pharisees, and second, in his references to himself as the Son of Man. The early Jesus uses the term publicly in a way that could only be offensive to most of his hearers. Then for a time he drops the public use and uses the name only in private before his disciples. When he next calls himself the Son of Man in public, he uses it vengefully against those who do not believe in him. Finally he calls himself the Son of Man triumphantly at his trial.

(1) Even before Jesus began teaching or working miracles, he called disciples. He saw Simon and his brother Andrew casting their net into the sea of Galilee, and he said to them, "Follow me, and I will make you fish for men" (Mark 1.17). He went along a

little further and saw James and John, sons of Zebedee, and immediately called them, and they followed him (1.19f.).

John's version, which is very different, also emphasizes Jesus' calling disciples. Two disciples of John followed Jesus—John had said Jesus was the Lamb of God—and asked where he was staying. Jesus replied, "Come, and see" (1.39). "The next day Jesus decided to go to Galilee. He found Phillip and said to him, 'Follow me'" (1.43).

John the Baptist had disciples, but we are not told that he actively recruited them. We know of no disciples of Isaiah, who resembles Jesus. All religious leaders seek followers; otherwise, their message has no point. But to seek out a close band of disciples who are very different from other followers is another matter and is typical of cult leaders. Throughout the Synoptics it is emphasized that the apostles are specially different from other followers of Jesus.

(2) Jesus began working miracles very early in his ministry (Mark 1.23ff.). In fact, Mark stresses his miracles more than the content of his message. Significantly, when Jesus was in his hometown, and people did not believe in him, he lost the ability to perform deeds of power (6.1ff.). Mark links conceptually the people's disbelief and Jesus' loss of power: "And he was amazed because of their unbelief" (6.6).

(3) Also from almost the beginning of his ministry Jesus confronted the institutional religious authorities, especially the Pharisees (2.1ff.). This escalating confrontation has already been set out in chapter 5. What has to be emphasized in the context of Jesus as a cult leader is that he confronted the religious authorities, not the secular rulers. Even after his execution the Romans did not pursue Jesus' followers.

(4) Again from an early point, Jesus taught in parables and incomprehensibly (4.3ff.). He meant his parables to be difficult to understand: "And he said, 'Let anyone with ears to hear listen'"

(4.19). Then he explained his meaning privately to his disciples—they too could not understand. More than that, he tells them that they have been given the secret of the kingdom of God but that he speaks in parables deliberately so that others will not understand, will not repent, and so will not be forgiven. This deliberate obscurity in meaning, couched in high rhetoric, continues throughout.

(5) Women had a special understanding of Jesus. The woman who had been hemorrhaging for twelve years touched his cloak and was healed (5.24ff.). Certainly this is not the first time Jesus cured someone who had faith in him. He had cured the leper who had said, "If you choose, you can make me clean" (1.40). And at this point he is on his way to cure the daughter of Jairus who had said, "My little daughter is at the point of death. Come and lay your hands on her, so that she may be made well, and live" (5.23). But the hemorrhaging woman is a different case. She does not tell Jesus of her faith in him, nor does she even ask him for a cure. Because of her faith she simply knows that if she touches his robe she will be cured. Her approach to Jesus is very different from that of the men.

Another woman who had a special understanding of Jesus was not even a Jew but a Gentile of Syrophoenician origin who had a daughter who was possessed (7.25ff.). She says nothing of her belief in Jesus but begs Jesus to cure her daughter. His reply is rough, crude, and offensive: "Let the children first be filled: for it is not good to take the children's bread, and throw it to the dogs" (7.27). For Jesus the children are the Jews, the dogs are the Gentiles. But the woman persists. She uses Jesus' terminology but in a soft, beseeching way: "Yes, Lord, and yet the dogs under the table eat the children's crumbs" (7.28). She accepts Jesus' view of the superiority of the Jews, even still refers to Gentiles as dogs, but insists they should not be totally overlooked. The woman has sufficient insight into Jesus to win him over.[2]

Shortly before his arrest, Jesus was at Bethany in the house of

Simon the leper when a woman anointed his head with very expensive ointment (14.3ff.). The ointment was worth more than three hundred *denarii:* a *denarius* was the usual day wage for a laborer, so the ointment represented a year's wages. The woman is not named or further described. This is the only act of loving kindness that we are told Jesus received in his lifetime. The woman's anonymity heightens this effect. Jesus was deeply moved and pleased.[3] In some very real sense she had understood his needs. This understanding is emphasized by the failure of the disciples: they were angry at the waste of money that could have been given to the poor.

When Jesus was crucified, his only followers who were present—so far as we are told—were women, according to Matthew 27.55f. and Mark 15.40f. Luke 23.49 records the presence of acquaintances including women. John 19.25 lists the mother of Jesus, her sister Mary, and Mary Magdalene, and a sole male—"the disciple whom he loved."

> Mark 15.40. There were also women looking on from a distance; among them were Mary Magdalene, and Mary the mother of James the younger and of Joses, and Salome. 41. These used to follow him and provided for him when he was in Galilee; and there were many other women who had come up with him to Jerusalem.

These women were showing sympathy. Mary Magdalene, the other Mary, and Salome had served Jesus in Galilee. Many other women were there who had followed him to Jerusalem. But Jesus seems to have lost the regard of his male disciples and of the men who had followed him to Jerusalem.[4]

Lastly, when the Sabbath was over, the two Marys and Salome were the ones who brought spices to the tomb to anoint Jesus' corpse.[5]

(6) Only at a relatively late point does Jesus reveal to his dis-

ciples that he must undergo great suffering, be rejected by the elders, the chief priests, and scribes, and be killed (8.31). This is a turning point for Jesus as leader of a cult. This is not at all what the disciples had expected. They are astonished. After all, Jesus has only just admitted to them that he is the Messiah. They do not comprehend. Peter rebukes him, and Jesus is furious. It is noteworthy that this is the first time in Mark that Jesus terms himself in private to his disciples "Son of Man."

Jesus also tells them at this point, in a fashion typical of a cult leader, that his death will not be the end and that after three days he will rise from the dead (8.31). Subsequently, he again tells them he will be betrayed, will be killed, and will be resurrected after three days (9.30ff.). The disciples' incomprehension is stressed. Again, on the way to Jerusalem Jesus foretells to his disciples in forthright language that he will be condemned and handed over to the Gentiles, who "will mock him, spit on him, flog him, and kill him; and after three days he will rise again" (10.33ff.).

In a very strong way Jesus insists that he will be persecuted and put to death while at the same time equally insisting that his death will not be the end but the beginning.

(7) Only once does Jesus call upon the populace at large to follow him:

> Mark 8.34. He called the crowd with his disciples, and said to them, "If any want to become my followers, let them deny themselves and take up their cross and follow me. 35. For those who want to save their life will lose it, and those who lose their life for my sake, and for the sake of the gospel, will save it. 36. For what will it profit them to gain the whole world and forfeit their life? 37. Indeed, what can they give in return for their life?"

This follows immediately upon his admitting to his disciples that he is the Messiah and telling them that he will suffer. Jesus' pronouncement to the crowd is typical of a cult leader, and it is multifaceted. Those who follow him will have to suffer, but they will have great reward. Those who do not follow him will suffer great vengeance. But there seems also to be a note of contempt. Jesus does not expect the crowd to follow him.

(8) Jesus shows particular interest in welcoming little children in his name at Mark 9.36f. and again at 42:

Mark 9.42. "If any of you put a stumbling block before one of these little ones who believe in me, it would be better for you if a great millstone were hung around your neck and you were thrown into the sea."

(9) In true cultic fashion Jesus will separate his followers from their families:

Mark 10.29. Jesus said, "Truly I tell you, there is no one who has left house or brothers or sisters or mother or father or children or fields, for my sake and for the sake of the good news, 30. who will not receive a hundredfold now in this age—houses, brothers and sisters, mothers and children, and fields with persecutions—and in the age to come eternal life. 31. But many who are first will be last, and the last will be first."

(10) Erratic and extreme mood swings are a feature of cult leaders: from loving benignity to unreasoning anger. A fine example is in Mark 11.12ff.

On the following day, when they came from Bethany, he was hungry. 13. Seeing in the distance a fig tree in leaf, he went to see whether perhaps he would find anything on it. When he came to it, he found nothing but leaves, for it was not the season for figs. 14. He said to it, "May no one ever eat fruit from you again." And his disciples heard it.

Jesus cursed the innocent fig tree—innocent, because it was not the season for figs. He did so because he was hungry and for no other reason that is mentioned. His behavior is quite irrational and unpleasant.[6]

> Mark 11.20. In the morning as they passed by, they saw the fig tree withered away to its roots. 21. Then Peter remembered and said to him, "Rabbi, look! The fig tree that you cursed has withered." 22. Jesus answered them, "Have faith in God. 23. Truly I tell you, if you say to this mountain, 'Be taken up and thrown into the sea,' and if you do not doubt in your heart, but believe that what you say will come to pass, it will be done for you. 24. So I tell you, whatever you ask for in prayer, believe that you have received it, and it will be yours."

No mention is made now of Jesus' hunger. Instead, he portrays his behavior as an act of power and faith in God. Still, nothing can change the fact that his act was destructive and would prevent others from benefiting from the tree at the right season.[7]

(11) As is typical of cult leaders, he predicts the apocalypse (13.14ff.). I do not want to stress this, because the coming of the apocalypse was also standard in visions of the Messiah. Still, there is a difference. In Mark, as is appropriate for a cult, the apocalypse is connected with the persecution of the leader's disciples.

In Mark, Jesus has the attributes of a cult leader. What must finally be stressed is what is lacking in Mark. Jesus has virtually no spiritual or theological message, a fact that makes the Gospel of Mark so different from Matthew and Luke. Papias of the second century tells us that Mark was a follower of Peter and "wrote down accurately, but not in order, as much as he [Peter] related of the sayings and doings of Christ."[8] Peter's vision of Jesus was that of what we regard as a cult leader.[9]

15
✠
CONCLUSIONS
✠ ✠ ✠

LITTLE CAN BE KNOWN ABOUT JESUS BEFORE HIS BAPTISM BY John. Myths about his birth abound, but they can be shown to be myths. More than that, we can tell how they arose. Joseph made the fictional trip to Bethlehem to fulfill the prophecy that the Messiah would be born there (Micah 5.2): the impossible tax obligation for Joseph was concocted to explain the trip. Herod's faked massacre of the innocents is to explain the Herodian hostility toward Jesus, thus downplaying John the Baptist,[1] and the flight to Egypt and the return are symbols of the Exodus.[2] The imaginary blood relationship with John is to account for Jesus' baptism by him and Jesus' continuance of John's teaching.[3] The impossible genealogy of Jesus from David through Joseph is to fulfill the belief that the Messiah will be the son of David. The story of the virgin birth is to fulfill with hindsight the prophecy of Isaiah that the great leader would have a virgin mother.[4]

What we can deduce is that Jesus was from Nazareth in Galilee, of undistinguished parentage. He may have been a carpenter, his mother was named Mary married to a man called Joseph, and he had brothers and sisters (Mark 6.3). At that time Galilee was not under direct Roman rule but was in the power of the puppet tetrarch, Herod Antipas. Nazareth was no more than a village. The Galileans were held in some contempt by the Pharisees because of their perceived lack of learning.

Jesus' baptism by John was the turning point. He immediately believed he was the one John was predicting: that he was the Son of God and incidentally—only incidentally—the Messiah. He immediately went into the desert for reflection and meditation. He remained there for forty days—a symbolic period chosen to reflect the Israelites' forty years in the wilderness after the Exodus. When he heard of John's arrest he immediately returned to Galilee and preached John's message but with a difference: the kingdom of God that John had predicted had now come.

Jesus, like John, preached repentance, and that was his main message. Only repentance would turn away the wrath of God. Hypocrisy was a great sin and was exemplified by the Pharisees. For Jesus, they observed outwardly, but their hearts were not with God. To show his authority Jesus used miracles, particularly miracles of healing and exorcism, right from the outset of his ministry. In this he was in contrast to John. At times, indeed, the miracles seem to take precedence over the message. Jesus believed he was beyond the law, but at first he was careful to be nonconfrontational. This quickly changed (in Mark, as early as chapter 2). At this stage he also openly proclaimed himself to be the Son of Man, by which he meant he was the Son of God. But soon he ceased to be so explicit.

At no point was Jesus interested in secular politics. He had no quarrel with the Romans, and the Romans had none with him. In this regard he did not resemble the awaited political Messiah.[5] Although Jesus believed he was the Messiah, that fact had little relevance to him whose call was for repentance by the Jews. Still, from the outset the supporters of Herod were extremely hostile. This was because of Jesus' connection with John the Baptist, whose call for repentance was thought likely to cause an uprising. Indeed, in this connection John railed against the unlawful marriage of Herod with his sister-in-law, Herodias, while her husband was yet alive. And Jesus not only was baptized by John but took up John's call for repentance when John was arrested.

Jesus recruited disciples and singled out twelve—not always the same twelve—who symbolized the twelve tribes of Israel. For them Jesus was the political Messiah, and it was of the political Messiah that they wanted to be disciples. This was one important factor in their prolonged misunderstanding of Jesus. This misunderstanding is stressed by Mark, and it is fundamental in explaining the disciples' lack of interest in most of Jesus' miracles—they were not the right kind—and their melting away when Jesus was arrested and seemed to be a failure. When Jesus appeared to them, resurrected, they again came to believe he was the political Messiah.

At first, the Pharisees were very interested in studying Jesus. They wanted to know if he was the Messiah; they probably also wondered if he was like them or could be co-opted. But they rapidly decided he was none of these. Not only did he show inattention to, even ignorance of, the law but he was also implacably hostile toward them. Jesus showed his hostility with ever-increasing violence.

An incidental but important conclusion also follows. Mark emerges as having considerable understanding of rabbinic—Pharisaical—thought. When Mark shows Jesus to be ignorant or careless of the law as viewed by the Pharisees, or to use unconvincing arguments about law, we must accept that this was a true part of the early tradition about Jesus and not the result of the evangelist's lack of knowledge.

To a great extent Jesus modeled himself on Isaiah, or on the prophet foretold by Isaiah, in a way that seems almost to have been deliberate. Once the similarities from copying are noticed, it is the differences that are most important. Thus, like the God of Isaiah, Jesus was untroubled by female religious uncleanliness. But Isaiah rails against female vanity in a way that to modern eyes appears hostile to women in a sexist fashion. In contrast, Jesus is attractive to women, they seem to understand him, and he responds positively to them. It is this that makes plausible the (now concealed) attack on Jesus in John's story of his encounter at Jacob's well with the woman of Samaria.[6] Again, Isaiah rails against the strict observance of the Sabbath and other festivals and against Temple sacrifices. Jesus is likewise hostile, but again the differences matter. Isaiah is hostile only because these observances take the place of the true worship of God, which, for him, is what counts. Jesus' opposition to the strict Sabbath observance and sacrifice is not expressly linked with his call to repentance. Jesus' opposition to Sabbath observance seems to be general dislike of the Pharisaic practices. And Jesus does not object verbally to Temple sacrifices. He deliberately physically sabotages them. Isaiah describes vividly the desolation that is to come in Israel when people fail to repent. Jesus also describes it vehemently, significantly on his way to Jerusalem where he expects to be persecuted and put to death. But in Jesus' version it appears that righteous and unrighteous alike will suffer. God told Isaiah to tell the people to hear but not understand, to see but not perceive. Isaiah's message is to be clear, but he is to tell the people that they will not understand. Jesus deliberately made his message one that the people could not understand: even his disciples failed to comprehend. Jesus' position—deliberate obfuscation—seems more extreme.

This deliberate obfuscation must be central to an understanding of Jesus. In Isaiah, it is the angry God who orders him to tell the people to hear but not understand. The tone is threatening. God is made to want vengeance. But beneath it all are the expectation of repentance and the desire for the people to repent. Isaiah is to tell the people they will hear but not understand. The point is to force them to seek understanding. But when Jesus claims that he speaks so that people will not understand, it appears that he is not seeking their repentance. This seems to me to be part of the true Jesus. It is this which makes possible the hostile Pharisaic source in John showing Jesus being cruel and unenlightening to the pure Nicodemus.[7] Certainly, there are other signs that Jesus wants people to repent. But a certain nastiness can scarcely be denied. In his parables he deliberately speaks so as not to be understood and so that the people will not repent.

There is a real problem here for believers. But there is no difficulty for those who perceive Jesus as a cult leader. Above all, a cult leader wants followers who believe he leads the way to salvation: he has no interest in the fate of the masses. Nor does he expect them to believe. Of course, faith in him is faith in his outstanding place in God's plan. Hence something more is needed. A standard feature of cult leaders is precisely their high-flown rhetoric, which is, and often seems intended to be, incomprehensible.

My portrait of Jesus is based very much on my reading of Mark, which more than the other Gospels seems to be true to the earliest traditions. I tend to believe the statement attributed to Papias by Eusebius, *Historia Ecclesiae* 3.39 (which I quoted in chapter 1) that the evangelist Mark became the interpreter of Peter. This I have not emphasized because I find no proof possible. But if it is accurate, then Mark is giving us Peter's vision of Jesus.[8] And Peter is recorded as having seen the resurrected Jesus and as believing he was the political Messiah.[9]

ABBREVIATIONS

✝ ✝ ✝

Anchor Bible Dictionary, 1–6	*The Anchor Bible Dictionary*, 6 vols., ed. David Noel Freedman (New York, 1992).
Brown, *Death*, 1, 2	Raymond E. Brown, *The Death of the Messiah,* 2 vols. (New York, 1994).
Daube, *New Testament*	David Daube, *The New Testament and Rabbinic Judaism* (London, 1956).
Grant, *Introduction*	Robert Grant, *A Historical Introduction to the New Testament* (London, 1963).
Historical Jesus	*The Historical Jesus: A Sheffield Reader*, ed. Craig A. Evans and Stanley E. Porter (Sheffield, 1995).
Mann, *Mark*	C. S. Mann, *Mark* (Garden City, N.Y. 1986).
Meier, *Marginal Jew*, 1, 2	John P. Meier, *A Marginal Jew*, 2 vols. (New York, 1991, 1994).

Messiah	*The Messiah: Developments in Earliest Judaism and Christianity,* ed. James H. Charlesworth (Minneapolis, 1992).
Mishnah	*The Mishnah,* trans. Herbert Danby (Oxford, 1933).
New Jerome	*The New Jerome Bible Commentary,* ed. Raymond E. Brown, Joseph A. Fitzmyer, and Roland E. Murphy (Englewood Cliffs, N.J., 1990).
Sanders, *Jesus*	E. P. Sanders, *The Historical Figure of Jesus* (London, 1993).
Strack-Billerbeck, *Kommentar,* 1, 2	Hermann L. Strack and Paul Billerbeck, *Kommentar zum Neuen Testament aus Talmud und Midrasch,* 1, 5th ed. (Munich, 1969); 2, 4th ed. (Munich, 1965).
Vermes, *Jesus the Jew*	Geza Vermes, *Jesus the Jew* (London, 1973).
Watson, *Jesus and the Jews*	Alan Watson, *Jesus and the Jews* (Athens, Ga., 1995).
Watson, *Jesus and the Law*	Alan Watson, *Jesus and the Law* (Athens, Ga., 1996).
Watson, *Stephen*	Alan Watson, *The Trial of Stephen: The First Christian Martyr* (Athens, Ga., 1996).
Watson, *Trial*	Alan Watson, *The Trial of Jesus* (Athens, Ga., 1995).

✛

NOTES

✛ ✛ ✛

PREFACE

1. For these see, e.g., Sanders, *Jesus,* 66ff., 118ff. For the background (and many other important matters) see, e.g., Sanders, *Jesus;* Meier, *Marginal Jew,* 1.

2. On the difficulty of reaching the truth, and the distinction between the "real Jesus" and the "historical Jesus," see, e.g., Meier, *Marginal Jew,* 1:21ff.

INTRODUCTION

1. For more on the historical background see, e.g., Vermes, *Jesus the Jew;* John Dominic Crossan, *The Historical Jesus* (San Francisco, 1991); Sanders, *Jesus.*

2. Josephus *Jewish Antiquities* 18.9ff.

3. Ibid., 18.12ff.

4. Ibid., 18.16f.

5. Ibid., 18.18ff.

6. Ibid., 18.23ff.

7. See, e.g., John 7.41, 52; cf. Vermes, *Jesus the Jew,* 52ff.

8. See, e.g., J. J. M. Roberts, "The Old Testament's Contribution to Messianic Expectations," in *Messiah,* 39ff.; P. D. Hanson "Messiahs and Messianic Figures in Proto-Apocalypticism" in *Messiah,* 67ff.; S. Talmon, "The Concepts of Māšîah and Messianism in Early Judaism," in *Messiah,* 79ff.; R. A. Horsley, "'Messianic' Figures and Movements in First-Century Palestine," in *Messiah,* 276ff. For a short account see Watson, *Trial,* 5ff.

9. Though it is not the purpose of the Gospels to give an account of Jesus' life. For a history of the Gospels, see, e.g., Sanders, *Jesus,* 58ff.

10. See, e.g., Watson, *Stephen,* 106ff.

11. David Daube, "A Prayer Pattern in Judaism," *Studia Evangelica* 73 (1959), 539ff.

12. For details see Daube, *New Testament,* 332ff. This view represents the standard commentary of the Babylonian Talmud Pesahim 120a. But Mishnah Pesahim 10.8 suggests that Passover meal ended when *all* fell asleep, and Rabbi Jose ben Halafta held it ended only when they fell into a deep sleep. The issue is immaterial in the present context.

13. David Daube, *Civil Disobedience in Antiquity* (Edinburgh, 1972), 112ff. Daube cites the sources.

14. I believe I owe this point to a conversation with Calum Carmichael.

15. It is also found in the Old Testament. For sources and a discussion see Daube, *New Testament,* 196ff.

16. See Daube, *New Testament,* 55ff.; cf. W. D. Davies, *The Setting of the Sermon on the Mount* (Cambridge, 1964), 101ff.

17. For the enormous literature on the Beatitudes see Meier, *Marginal Jew,* 2:377n. 12.

18. See, e.g., Watson, *Jesus and the Jews,* 4ff. and the works cited.

19. Meier, *Marginal Jew,* 1:171ff.

20. Josephus *Jewish Antiquities* 18.136.

21. An attempt at a reconstruction is set out by Harold W. Hoehner in *The International Standard Bible Encyclopedia,* ed. Geoffrey W. Bromiley (Grand Rapids, 1982), 2:693.

22. See, e.g., the discussion in Harold W. Hoehner, *Herod Antipas* (Cambridge, 1972), 131ff.

23. This is admitted by Meier, *Marginal Jew,* 1:172.

24. Josephus *Jewish Antiquities* 18.119.

25. Josephus *Jewish War* 2.43.

1 "AND THE LARGE CROWD WAS LISTENING TO HIM WITH DELIGHT"

1. Walter W. Wessel, in *Zondervan NIV Bible Commentary,* ed. Kenneth L. Barker and John Kohlenberger (Grand Rapids, 1994), 2:185.

2. David Daube, "The Earliest Structure of the Gospels," *New Testament Studies* 5 (1958–59): 174ff.

3. Each husband, we are told, dies without producing a child: that is, the marriages are levirate.

4. Vincent Taylor, *The Gospel according to St. Mark* (London, 1953), 490.

5. C. E. B. Cranfield, *The Gospel according to Saint Mark* (Cambridge, 1972), 381f.

6. Mann, *Mark,* 483.

7. Daube, "Earliest Structure," 174ff.

8. See Watson, *Trial,* 143ff.

9. For this part of the liturgy see *The Passover Haggadah,* ed. Nahum N. Glatzer (New York, 1953), 29ff.

10. Ibid., 35. For this point see Daube, "Earliest Structure."

11. But Luke, which omits the third question in this context, puts the fear to ask another question in front of Jesus' question about the son of David: 20.40.

12. Daube, *New Testament,* 166ff.

13. See Daube, "Earliest Structure," 181.

14. Eusebius does not record why Mark changed the order of events he heard from Peter. Or does Eusebius mean, as the second sentence of the translation might suggest, that it was only Peter who changed the order?

15. Infra, chap. 6.

16. Various solutions have been offered: see the works cited by Bruce Chilton, "Jesus *ben David:* Reflections on the *Davidssohnfrage,*" in *Historical Jesus,* 192ff.; D. H. Juel, "The Origin of Mark's Christology," in *Messiah,* 453ff.

17. See, e.g., Daniel J. Harrington in *New Jerome,* 622.

2 JOHN THE BAPTIST

1. For the historical existence of John see Meier, *Marginal Jew,* 2:19ff., 56ff.

2. See, e.g., Sanders, *Jesus,* 92f.

3. Josephus *Jewish Antiquities* 18.109–13.

4. Cf. Luke 3.19f.

5. Deuteronomy 25.5.

6. Josephus *Jewish Antiquities* 18.109. As we saw in my introduction, which brother is a matter of dispute but need not detain us.

7. For John's moral directives see, e.g., Meier, *Marginal Jew,* 2:40ff.

8. See Daube, *New Testament,* 106ff.; on the nature of John's baptizing see also Meier, *Marginal Jew,* 2:49ff.

9. Matthew 3.1ff.; Mark 1.4; Luke 3.3. In private correspondence Ranon Katzoff suggests that baptism by John would make one a *chaver,* a member of a group, and that when Jesus, as a *chaver,* ate with *am ha'aretz,* thus probably making his food unclean, he would violate his commitment as a *chaver.*

10. Josephus *Jewish War* 2.123.

11. Cf., e.g., Grant, *Introduction,* 310. This is so even if one holds his diet of locusts and wild honey was chosen for reasons of ritual purity. John's disciples fasted (Matthew 9.14; Luke 5.33) whereas Jesus' did not. Cf. Luke 7.3ff. For a discussion of the significance of John's diet and clothing see Meier, *Marginal Jew,* 2:46ff.

12. John's vituperation specifically against Pharisees and Sadducees in Matthew 3.7 has no counterpart in Mark.

13. At John 1.19ff. John the Baptist is made to say that he is neither the Messiah nor Elijah.

14. Matthew 3.13ff.; Mark 1.9; Luke 3.21.

15. See, e.g., Meier, *Marginal Jew,* 2:116ff.

16. For a discussion see Meier, *Marginal Jew,* 2:100ff.

17. See also Matthew 4.12; Luke 4.14.

18. See Matthew 4.23ff.; Mark 1.21ff.; Luke 4.14ff.

19. See also Jesus' question about John at Luke 20.1ff.

20. The tradition is implausible because Herod, as tetrarch of Galilee, has no jurisdiction in Judaea where Jesus' supposed offenses were committed. The story is made up to emphasize Pilate's reluctance to condemn Jesus.

21. See in general, Meier, *Marginal Jew,* 2:19ff.

3 JESUS BEFORE HIS MINISTRY

1. On Herod see, e.g., L. I. Levine in *Anchor Bible Dictionary,* 3:161ff.

2. In *New Jerome* 636. Sanders thinks the slaughter is unlikely: *Jesus,* 87.

3. But Daube is tempted to see an analogy of Herod with Laban in the Passover Midrash: both are at the same time an alien and related; both want to kill all the infants (not, like Pharaoh, only the males): *New Testament,* 189f.

4. See, e.g., Raymond E. Brown, *The Birth of the Messiah,* 2d ed. (New York, 1993), 505ff; cf. Grant, *Introduction,* 303f. On the issue in general see Meier, *Marginal Jew,* 1:208ff., 216ff.

5. The *Protevangelium of James* 10.1 tries to get around this issue by making Mary of the tribe of David: the text is in J. K. Elliott, *The Apocryphal New Testament* (Oxford, 1993), 61. But Jewish genealogy is traced through the husband.

6. See in general, Meier, *Marginal Jew,* 1:214ff.

7. For Quirinius, see, e.g., the overview by C. L. Blomberg in *The International Standard Bible Encyclopedia,* 3d ed., ed. Geoffrey W. Bromiley et al. (Grand Rapids, Mich., 1988), 4:12f.

8. Oddly, Grant believes an earlier census is possible: *Introduction*, 304.

9. We can generally ignore the testimony of the apocryphal Infancy Gospels. On the conflicting birth stories see also Sanders, *Jesus*, 85ff.

10. For the precedence of Mark in time—a different issue—see, e.g., Meier, *Marginal Jew*, 1:43ff.

11. I have said nothing about the account in Luke 2.41ff.—and only in Luke—of Jesus going with his parents each year to Jerusalem for Passover or remaining behind when he was twelve to dispute in the Temple. That they would go every year to celebrate Passover is plausible. That an early Christian tradition would evolve that even as a young boy Jesus would debate with the learned is not surprising. I neglect the account in Luke simply because the totality of evidence shows that the gospel writers had no hard evidence for Jesus before his baptism. But Grant, for example, points out that for Luke the source of the tradition was Mary: *Introduction*, 308f.

12. For the way stories might arise about the life of Jesus, cf. Sanders, *Jesus*, 58f., 62f.

4 JESUS AND JOHN THE BAPTIST

1. My understanding of the impact of this baptism is among the approaches that Meier regards as "hopelessly naive": *Marginal Jew*, 2:100ff. But I believe it is fully in harmony with the evidence.

2. See, e.g., the discussion in Meier, *Marginal Jew*, 1:168f.

3. See Sanders, *Jesus*, 112ff. I would suspect that the real temptation for Jesus would be to renounce his role as the Son of God. Jesus' answers to the devil would show this in allegory: Matthew 4.1ff.

4. See Meier, *Marginal Jew*, 1:41f., 252ff.

5 JESUS AND THE LAW

1. *Mishnah*, 452n. 13.

2. Steven F. Friedell kindly points out in a private letter: "Menahem Meiri (1249–1316 Provence) in his commentary to Aboth suggests a

meaning like yours not only for "gematria" but for the entire saying. He says that "bird offerings" refers to the Mishnah's tractate "Kinnim" at the end of the Order Kodashim and "the onset of menstruation" refers to the tractate "Niddah" in the last Order Toharot. These are not only difficult topics but since they come at the end of the Mishnah, R. Eleazar Hisma is in effect saying that one must study the Mishnah from beginning to end before studying worldly wisdom and divine matters."

3. I argue this from the fact that "leaning" of hands on a sacrificial animal on a feast day was regarded by the followers of Shamai—the followers of Hillel disagreed—as using an animal on a feast day which was forbidden: Mishnah Betzah 2.4; Mishnah Hagigah 2.2f.; Babylonian Talmud Betzah 20a; Babylonian Talmud Hagigah 16b. Laying on of hands as a blessing is a different case: Mishnah Tamid 7.2. Jesus' act is of healing, not blessing.

4. The repetition is absent from Matthew 8.16 and Luke 4.40.

5. This is so even if the respect was for them to avoid carrying on the Sabbath. But then the emphasis, by repetition, that the Sabbath had ended seems misplaced.

6. In general for Jesus' miracles and exorcisms see, e.g., Meier, *Marginal Jew,* 2:435ff., 617ff., 646ff.

7. Mishnah Demai 2.3: cf., e.g., Watson, *Jesus and the Law,* 33ff.

8. On fasting see, e.g., Meier, *Marginal Jew,* 2:439ff.

9. Mishnah Shabbat 7.2.

10. Even if there was only a suspicion that the life was in danger: Mishnah Yoma 8.6.

11. I have tried to bring this out in detail in *Jesus and the Law.*

12. The legal point is also often lost in modern discussions: e.g., G. D. Kilpatrick, "Jesus, his Family and his Disciples," in *Historical Jesus,* 13ff. It should be noticed that Jesus' family were not among his followers during his lifetime: cf., e.g., Sanders, *Jesus,* 125f.

13. See, e.g. Claude G. Montefiore, *The Synoptic Gospels* (New York, 1968), 1:148.

14. For the concept see, e.g., Perry Dane, "The Oral Law and the Jurisprudence of a Textless Text," *S'vara* (1991) 11ff.

15. See, e.g., E. P. Sanders, *Jewish Law from Jesus to the Mishnah* (Philadelphia, 1990), 5: "The prohibition of divorce . . . is radical . . . but it is not against the law, since staying married is not a transgression."

16. For a fuller treatment of Jesus' strange pronouncements on divorce see Watson, *Jesus and the Law*, 68ff.

17. I say "precincts" because selling in the Temple itself is unthinkable.

18. See, Mishnah Shekalim.

19. See, e.g., Watson, *Jesus and the Law*, 81ff. In fact, Jesus' contacts with Gentiles would be slight. In the Gospels he only once refers to a Gentile practice (Matthew 6.7): cf. Louis H. Feldman in *Christianity and Rabbinic Judaism*, ed. Hershel Shanks (Washington, D.C., 1992), 22.

20. See, e.g., Watson, *Jesus and the Law*, 68ff.

21. Unless one says that their claim that Jesus was the Messiah was the crime of leading a whole town astray: Mishnah Sanhedrin 7.9.

22. See now, e.g., Watson, *Stephen*, 120.

23. See, e.g., Acts 22.3, 23.6.

6 MARK 7.19

1. But for notions of work see Exodus 16, 35.2f.; Numbers 15.32ff.

2. Mark 10.5; Matthew 19.8: cf. David Daube, "Concessions to Sinfulness in Jewish Law," *Journal of Jewish Studies* 10 (1959): 1ff., now in David Daube, *Collected Works*, vol. 1, *Talmudic Law* (Berkeley, 1992), 1ff.

3. Cf. Matthew 5.31. In these texts *adultery* should not be treated as a technical legal term.

4. E. P. Sanders, *Jewish Law from Jesus to the Mishnah* (Philadelphia, 1990), 28.

5. In *New Jerome*, 612, Harrington refers to Galatians 2.11–14; Romans 14.14–20; Colossians 2.20–23; Acts 10.14–15.

6. See, e.g., C. H. Dodd, *The Founder of Christianity* (London, 1970), 74; Heikki Räisänen, *Jesus, Paul, and Torah*, trans. David E. Orton (Sheffield, 1992), 127ff.

7. Mann, *Mark,* 315.

8. See Vermes, *Jesus the Jew,* 29.

9. See Watson, *Jesus and the Law.*

10. A *pondion* was the smallest silver coin.

11. See, e.g., Danby, *Mishnah,* 616n. 2.

12. Mishnah Parah 7.5.

13. Mishnah Parah 8.7.

14. See, e.g., Jacob Neusner, *The Mishnah: A New Translation* (New Haven, 1988), xvff.

15. See, e.g., Brown, *Death,* 1:123. Cf. Calum M. Carmichael, *The Story of Creation* (Ithaca, 1996), 39n. 16.

16. See Leviticus 2.13–21.

17. See, e.g., the discussion by Haym Soloveitchic, "Rupture and Reconstruction: The Transformation of Contemporary Orthodoxy," *Tradition* 28 (1994): 64ff.

18. Mann, *Mark,* 315.

19. Ibid., 317.

20. See, e.g., W. Robertson Nicoll, *The Expositor's Greek Testament* (Grand Rapids, Mich., 1970), 1:389; Vincent Taylor, *The Gospel according to St. Mark* (London, 1953), 345; Robert G. Bratcher, *A Translator's Handbook on the Gospel of Mark* (Leiden, 1961), 232.

21. See, e.g., Sherman E. Johnson, *A Commentary on the Gospel according to St. Mark* (New York, 1960), 134.

22. See, e.g., Maurya P. Horgan in *New Jerome,* 877.

7   THE TRIAL OF JESUS

1. Cf. Brown, *Death,* 1:247.

2. On the young man see ibid., 1:294ff.

3. Cf. ibid., 1:433f.

4. On this see Daube, "Judas," *Rechtshistorisches Journal* 13 (1994): 21.

5. This statement is made despite Mishnah Sanhedrin 7.5. For the argument see Watson, *Jesus and the Law,* 29ff., 41ff., and later in this chapter.

6. Cf. Leviticus 10.6f. In private correspondence Ranon Katzoff produces a different explanation for the high priest tearing his garments. It is at least as plausible (though more has to be read into the episode) and more learned than mine. I give it in full:

> Second, as you observe the definition of blasphemy given by the Mishna Sanhedrin 7.5 is extremely restrictive, so much so as to make prosecution for blasphemy nearly an academic matter. Jesus' utterance that evening certainly would not fall under the Mishna's definition of blasphemy.
>
> I suggest, then, that a plausible explanation of some of the events of the evening would run along the following lines. The elders generally agree that Jesus must be gotten rid of. The problem is to get a technical capital charge to stick despite slippery witnesses. Caiaphas suggests charging him with blasphemy uttered in their presence. Let us now suppose that the restrictive definition of blasphemy was already the accepted one, but not so set in stone that it would be inconceivable to attempt an extensive interpretation. Caiaphas, then, proposes that the definition of blasphemy can be broader and leads Jesus into saying something which falls under Caiaphas's broader definition of blasphemy. Caiaphas must then immediately rend his clothes, not as a sign of mourning, nor because the accused has been condemned, but because he has just heard blasphemy, according to his definition, uttered in his presence. The other elders, despite their eagerness to be rid of Jesus, are not convinced by Caiaphas's extensive definition of blasphemy, and hence do not rend their clothes, because by their rights (as by the Mishna's) Jesus' statement does not fall under the definition of blasphemy. They nonetheless think he deserves death, but had as yet found no way to do anything about it.
>
> Caiaphas's point in 14.63 that they need no more witnesses is interesting. Rabbinic jurisprudence has this principle, that if an event—a crime, a transaction, a natural occurrence—the classic examples are murder, dispositions by someone on his deathbed, and the new moon—took place in the presence of a court, the

court may act on that without further witnesses. "Hearing should not be greater than seeing." However, this applies only if the court was in legal session (or could be. The last detail is definitely the law, though my son and I spent hours trying unsuccessfully to rationalize that). If the judges could not have been in legal session at the time they saw the event, then when they later are in legal session, witnesses to the event are required for the court to take any action. The main pericopes on this in the Babylonian Talmud are Rosh Hashana 25b-26a, Bava Kama 90b (both mostly tannaitic); Bava Batra 113b-114a, Ketubot 21b (both mostly amoriaic). So Caiaphas invokes the rule of "hearing should not be greater," but is stymied by the fact that it is night and not a legal session. Even an attempt to revive it in the morning would fail, because witnesses to the blasphemy would still be required.

Incidentally, the high priest is enjoined from tearing his garment in mourning, but not for other motives.

7. Cf. Brown, *Death,* 1:679ff.

8. Josephus *Jewish War* 2.218.

9. It is, of course, possible that Simon acquired the nickname before he became a disciple of Jesus. Then at the least the nickname would tell us nothing about Jesus' attitude to Zealots, but its very retention would still suggest that Jesus' group were not revolutionaries.

10. The argument is that early Christians were embarrassed in the Roman Empire that their God was an enemy of Rome, so they cut out all evidence. But his execution by the Romans, not the Jews, kept in the tradition would be just as embarrassing.

11. We need not consider here the extent to which the passage is not genuine Josephus, but see Watson, *Jesus and the Jews,* 15f.

12. The Suetonius passage is *Divus Claudius* 25.4.

13. This appears from the fact that the high priest's robes were kept in a stone chamber in the Roman fortress, the Antonia, under a triple seal, one being that of the Roman commander: Josephus *Jewish Antiquities* 15.403ff., 18.90ff., 20.6f; cf. Sanders, *Jesus,* 26f.

14. Cf., e.g., D. Cohen and C. Paulus, "Einige Bemerkungen zum

Prozess Jesu bei den Synoptikern," *Zeitschrift der Savigny Stiftung (romanistische Abteilung)* 102 (1985): 437ff. at 445f.

15. The hesitations that are sometimes expressed, e.g., by Brown, *Death,* 1:710ff., of the nature of the trial by Pontius Pilate are quite unfounded. It must be remembered that Jesus was not a Roman citizen. For a clear account of the powers of trial and execution of governors such as Pilate see A. N. Sherwin-White, *Roman Society and Roman Law in the New Testament* (Oxford, 1963), 1ff., 24ff. In most matters Roman criminal law did not change quickly: see, e.g., O. F. Robinson, *The Criminal Law of Ancient Rome* (Baltimore, 1995), ix.

16. I believe it was, following G. E. M. de Ste. Croix, "Why Were the Early Christians Persecuted?" *Past and Present* 26 (1963): 6ff.; "Why Were the Early Christians Persecuted?—a Rejoinder," *Past and Present* 27 (1964): 28ff.

17. See, e.g., A. N. Sherwin-White, *Oxford Classical Dictionary,* 2d ed. (Oxford, 1970), 846f.

18. See, e.g., A. M. Rabello, "Jewish and Roman Jurisdiction," in *An Introduction to the History and Sources of Jewish Law,* ed. N. S. Hecht et al. (Oxford, 1996), 142ff.

19. For the argument that the Sanhedrin had the power to put to death see Watson, *Trial,* 100ff., and later in this chapter. The only evidence to the contrary is John 18.31, which is effectively contradicted by the beginning of that verse, and John 19.6. In Babylonian Talmud Shabbat 15a there is a tradition that the Sanhedrin stopped hearing criminal cases forty years before the destruction of the Temple.

20. The account in John is internally consistent. It is not surprising that Sanders finds it the most satisfactory version: *Jesus,* 67.

21. See, Brown, *Death,* 1:389.

22. Strack and Billerbeck take the High Priest's words as putting Jesus on oath: *Kommentar,* 1:1005f. But see David Daube, "Judas," *Rechtshistorisches Journal* 13 (1994): 20f.

23. Cf. David Daube, "Judas," *California Law Review* 82 (1994): 95ff.

24. Mishnah Makkoth 1.6 records a dispute between the Sadducees and the Sages (i.e., Pharisees). The Sadducees held that a perjurer could

be put to death only after the person falsely accused had been executed. The Sages' view was that a perjurer could be put to death after the judges heard his false testimony but before the convicted person was executed. Deuteronomy 19.18 clearly supports the stance of the Sages, and this will be the older view: cf. David Daube, *Studies in Biblical Law* (Cambridge, 1947), 129.

The legal issue is enormously complicated. Judas' wicked behavior was not obviously the bearing of false evidence but betraying a fellow Jew (indeed, his teacher) to hostile authorities and ultimately to an occupying foreign power, and this is an act equally justifying the death penalty.

For us, what really matters in this context is not the precise nature of Judas' offense but that Matthew 27.3 expressly tells us that it was because Jesus was condemned that Judas brought back the thirty pieces of silver and hanged himself.

25. See Brown, *Death,* 1:389f.

26. Pilate certainly had jurisdiction. On *forum delicti* or *forum domicilii* see Sherwin-White, *Roman Society,* 28ff. For other explanations of Pilate's behavior see Joseph A. Fitzmyer, *The Gospel according to Luke X–XXIV* (Garden City, N.Y., 1985), 1478ff.

27. Cf., e.g., Cohen and Paulus, "Einige Bemerkungen" (1985), 448ff.

28. See, e.g., Strack-Billerbeck, *Kommentar* 1:1006.

29. David Daube, "Judas," *California Law Review* 82 (1994): 95ff., at 102.

30. Fitzmyer sees real political character in this accusation; perverting the nation, he says, is specifically obstructing the payment of taxes to Caesar and claiming to be an anointed king: *John X–XXIV,* 1473. This is unconvincing. The charge that Jesus claimed to be a king is a separate accusation: even there it is a subordinate charge. And why not simply and specifically claim he was obstructing the payment of taxes?

31. But see Watson, *Trial,* 119ff.

32. See, e.g., Josephus *Jewish War* 2.169ff.; Josephus *Jewish Antiquities* 18.35, 55ff., 85ff., 95; Philo *Embassy to Gaius* 301.

33. On the whole issue see now Watson, *Jesus and the Law,* 41ff.

34. But let me insist again that no other religious crime would fit the charge against Jesus.

35. See, e.g., A. J. Saldanini in *Anchor Bible Dictionary*, 5:978; Brown, *Death*, 1:343ff.

36. See, e.g., Emil Schürer, *The History of the Jewish People in the Age of Jesus Christ (175 B.C.–A.D. 135)*, 2d ed., ed. Geza Vermes, Fergus Millar, Matthew Black, Martin Goodmar, and Pamela Vermes (Edinburgh, 1979), 2:210.

37. For the issue see now Watson, *Trial*, 100ff.

38. See now Watson, *Jesus and the Jews*, 47f., 103f.

39. Philo, *Embassy to Gaius* 212, 307. The evidence is for A.D. 39 or 40.

40. Josephus *Jewish War* 6.124. The evidence is for A.D. 70.

41. Josephus *Jewish Antiquities* 20.200.

42. I leave aside the stoning of Stephen because this was a lynching even though preceded by a trial: Acts 6.11ff., 7.54ff.

43. Watson, *Trial*, 100f.; Watson, *Jesus and the Jews*, 84.

44. Origen, *On Romans* 6.7.

45. Watson, *Trial*, 104. Babylonian Talmud Avoda Zara 8.2 relates that forty years before the destruction of the Temple the Sanhedrin stopped hearing capital cases. In light of the other evidence I would suggest that this is part of the idealizing process already noted in the Mishnah where blasphemy has a very restricted sense and Sadducees are not judges.

8 MIRACLES, TEACHING, AND PARABLES

1. Cf. Sanders, *Jesus*, 128, 132.

2. James Strong, *The New Strong's Exhaustive Concordance of the Bible* (Nashville, 1990). For miracles in general see Meier, *Marginal Jew*, 2:509ff., 535ff.

3. See Daube, *New Testament*, 205f.

4. See also Matthew 13.54ff.; Mark 6.1ff.

5. Matthew 13.58; Mark 6.5.

6. See, e.g., Meier, *Marginal Jew*, 2:535ff.

7. See, e.g., Euripides *Bacchae* 704ff.; Athenaeus *Learned Banquet* 1.34a; Pausanias *Description of Greece* 6.261f.

8. See, e.g., C. K. Barrett, *The Gospel according to St. John*, 2d ed. (Philadelphia, 1978), 188.

9. Suetonius *Divus Vespasianus*, 7; Tacitus *Historiae* 4.81; Dio Cassius 65.8.

10. *Jewish Antiquities* 18.63f. The text is widely held to be corrupt, but the standard reconstruction retains Jesus as a miracle worker. See, e.g., Watson, *Trial*, 15f. For a good account of ancient miracles see Sanders, *Jesus*, 132ff.

11. Origen *Contra Celsum* 1.47, and *Commentarius in Matthaeum* 13.55.

12. I believe Jesus' religious and moral teaching is understressed in Mark because the apostles—Mark is thought to be the follower of Peter—were interested in Jesus as the political Messiah. When he turned out not to be so, the focus of attention of early Christians shifted to other aspects of his message.

9 JESUS AND THE MESSIAH

1. Matthew 26.26; Mark 14.22; Luke 22.19.

2. David Daube, *He that Cometh* (St. Paul's Lecture, London, 1966), 13.

3. Ibid., 6ff. He had a forerunner in Robert Eisler, "Das letzte Abendmahl," *Zeitschrift für die Neutestamentliche Wissenschaft* 24 (1925): 161ff. Cf. D. B. Carmichael, "David Daube on the Eucharist and the Passover Seder," *Journal for the Study of the New Testament* 42 (1991): 45ff.

4. For the argument see Watson, *Stephen*, 3ff.: see also Louis H. Feldman in *Christianity and Rabbinic Judaism*, ed. Hershel Shanks (Washington, D.C., 1992), 7.

5. For the argument see Watson, *Stephen*, 78ff.

6. For Jesus the Messiah who was very different from the expected

Messiah see, e.g., J. H. Charlesworth, "From Messianology to Christology," in *Messiah*, 3ff.; cf. B. L. Mack, "The Christ and Jewish Wisdom," in *Messiah*, 192ff.; J. D. G. Dunn, "Messianic Ideas and Their Influence on the Jesus of History," in *Messiah*, 365ff.

10   JESUS AND THE SON OF MAN

1. For other views see, e.g., Richard Bauckham, "The Son of Man: 'A Man in my Position' or 'Someone,'" in *Historical Jesus*, 245ff. For the well-known problem of the terminology see also F. H. Borsch, "Further Reflections on 'the Son of Man,'" in *Messiah*, 130ff.

2. In Mark: Matthew 9.2ff. and Luke 4.17ff. are different, but their construct is illogical. They (in Luke, Pharisees and scribes) *said* "he blasphemes," but Jesus read their *thoughts*. For the full argument see Watson, *Jesus and the Law*, 26ff.

3. Vermes, *Jesus the Jew*, 160ff., especially 183.

4. See, e.g., D. E. Aune, s.v. "Son of Man," in *The International Standard Bible Encyclopedia*, rev. ed. (Grand Rapids, 1988), 4:574ff.

5. *The New Revised Standard Version* has "like a human being."

6. See the treatment by Aune, "Son of Man," 574f.

7. Luke's account is confused: 22.66ff., 23.1ff. Of course, some scholars—see the references in Aune, "Son of Man," 580—deny the authenticity of all Jesus' sayings on this. My concern is with the tradition in Mark and its author's vision.

8. Cf. Luke 9.58.

9. Cf. Luke 7.34.

11   JESUS AS OTHERS SAW HIM

1. Cf. Vermes, *Jesus the Jew*, 129ff.

2. See, e.g., Daube, *New Testament*, 208f.

3. See, e.g., Sanders, *Jesus*, 120ff., 291.

4. Daniel J. Harrington, in *New Jerome*, 611.

5. Certainly John had disciples and did not claim that he was the Messiah. But he did claim that the more powerful one would come after him, a claim totally absent from Jesus' message.

6. On the meaning of a "sign" see, e.g., Jeffrey Gibson, "Jesus' Refusal to Produce a 'Sign' (Mark 8.11–13)," in *Historical Jesus,* 271ff.

7. See, e.g., Mann, *Mark,* 322ff.; Harrington, in *New Jerome,* 613.

8. At Mark 7.37 "they" were astounded. "They" refers not to the disciples but to the people: cf. Taylor, *St. Mark,* 356.

9. See, e.g., Strack-Billerbeck, *Kommentar,* 1: 845; Vincent Taylor, *The Gospel according to St. Mark* (London, 1953), 456. W. F. Albright and C. S. Mann take *hosanna* in its original meaning and not as a cry of praise: *Matthew* (New York, 1971), 252.

10. This approach was not strictly observed: see the instances in Strack-Billerbeck, *Kommentar,* 2:26.

11. In a letter to me, Steven F. Friedell produces an additional perspective which I have set out in Watson, *Trial,* 189n. 26.

12 JESUS AND ISAIAH

1. A rather different view is that of John F. A. Sawyer, *The Fifth Gospel: Isaiah in the History of Christianity* (Cambridge, 1996), 35f.

2. See also, e.g., Isaiah 1.26f.

3. We should not ignore Jeremiah.

4. When Hezekiah began to reign, he also cleansed the Temple but in an essentially nonviolent way: 2 Chronicles 29.3ff.

5. Cf. Matthew 24.1ff.; Luke 21.5ff.

6. See also, e.g., Isaiah 1.23, 10.1ff., and 41.17ff.

13 MARK AND PROPHECIES

1. For prophecies shaping the status of Jesus see, e.g., D. E. Aune, "Christian Prophecy and the Messianic Status of Jesus," in *Messiah,* 404ff.

2. It should be noted, though, that the Hebrew "young woman" is

not the technical term for a virgin, and "virgin" may not have been Isaiah's meaning: cf., e.g., Joseph Jensen in *New Jerome,* 235.

3. See, e.g., Daniel J. Harrington in *New Jerome* 615.

4. Cf. Mark 8.31.

14 JESUS, THE LEADER OF A CULT

1. Based on Alexander Deutsch, "Psychological Perspectives on Cult Leadership," in *Cult and New Religious Movements,* ed. Marc Galanter (Washington, 1989), 147–57. See also, e.g., Leon Festinger, Henry W. Riecken, and Stanley Schacter, *When Prophecy Fails* (Minneapolis, 1956), 1ff.; Willa Appel, *Cults in America: Programmed for Paradise* (New York, 1983), 38ff.

2. On the Syrophoenician woman see Meier, *Marginal Jew,* 2:563n. 36, 659ff.

3. We need not suppose that the woman intended to anoint his body beforehand for burial, although that is Jesus' explanation.

4. For women who supported Jesus and his disciples see, e.g., Sanders, *Jesus,* 109f., 124f.

5. In Mark (as in the other Synoptics) there is no Nicodemus who anoints Jesus.

6. Instructive is, for example, the treatment by Daniel J. Harrington in *New Jerome,* 619, who suggests that Mark transformed a story into a parable.

7. For unconvincing theological explanations see Meier, *Marginal Jew,* 2:641ff., 887ff.

8. Eusebius, *Historia Ecclesiae* 3.39: quoted in chapter 1.

9. There is no equivalent in Mark of Matthew 16.17ff.

15 CONCLUSIONS

1. But see also the prophecy in Jeremiah 31.15.

2. See also Hosea 11.1.

3. For a forerunner to Jesus see Isaiah 40.3ff.; Malachi 3.1.

4. Isaiah 7.14. On the whole issue see, e.g., Meier, *Marginal Jew,* 1:220ff.

5. It is appropriate to call attention to the famous text about Jesus that appears in the Slavonic, but not the Greek, version of Josephus's *Jewish War.* The text shows an awareness of a tradition about his followers: "When they saw his ability to do whatever he wished by a word, they told him that they wanted him to enter the city, destroy the Roman troops, and make himself king: but he took no notice." This view of Jesus is echoed in John 6.15: "When Jesus realized that they were about to come and take him by force to make him king, he withdrew again to the mountain by himself." On the significance of the whole passage see Watson, *Trial of Jesus,* 128ff. Meier rejects the passage as unauthentic because it "is a wildly garbled condensation of various Gospel events, seasoned with the sort of bizarre legendary expansions found in apocryphal gospels and acts of the 2d and 3d centuries" (*Marginal Jew,* 1:57). But it is precisely the awareness of different traditions in the text that incline me to accept it as genuine Josephus.

6. See Watson, *Jesus and the Jews,* 29ff.

7. See ibid., 38ff.

8. I have said nothing about the place of composition or dating of Mark because I do not find the arguments compelling for Rome before A.D. 70.

9. Acts 1.6ff., 13, 22, 2.14ff., 3.11ff., 4.1ff.

✠

INDEX OF TEXTS

✠ ✠ ✠

1 OLD TESTAMENT

2 NEW TESTAMENT

3 RABBINIC SOURCES

4 CLASSICAL SOURCES